THE QUEEN AND THE HERETIC

"Derek Wilson has written a fine history of two little-known and controversial women as thinkers. Though one is a queen of Henry VIII and the other is a martyr, they appear on the pages as lively, complex, realistic women — far from the stereotypes of traditional history.

Wilson has traced their connections and carefully judged their intimacy. His understanding of the cliques which attached themselves to Henry VIII and his last wife is detailed and careful — authentic history — while never losing sight of the nightmarish atmosphere of a court governed by a bad-tempered tyrant."

PHILIPPA GREGORY, historian and author

THE QUEEN
AND THE HERETIC

*How two women changed the
religion of England*

DEREK WILSON

LION

Published by
Lion Hudson Limited
Wilkinson House, Jordan Hill Business Park,
Banbury Road, Oxford OX2 8DR, England
www.lionhudson.com

Hardback ISBN 978 0 7459 6880 3
Paperback ISBN 978 0 7459 6882 7
e-ISBN 978 0 7459 6881 0

First edition 2018

Cover acknowledgments

Background: The burning of Anne Askew at Smithfield © Lebrecht Music and Arts Photo Library/Alamy Stock Photo; Catherine Parr © Granger Historical Picture Archive/Alamy Stock Photo

Text acknowledgments

Extracts from The Authorized (King James) Version. Rights in the Authorized Version are vested in the Crown. Reproduced by permission of the Crown's patentee, Cambridge University Press.

Scriptures quotations marked GNB are from the Good News Bible © 1994 published by the Bible Societies/HarperCollins Publishers Ltd UK, Good News Bible © American Bible Society 1966, 1971, 1976, 1992. Used with permission.

pp. 5–6: Quoted material from Collected Works of Erasmus – Colloquies, volume 39, translated by C. Thompson © University of Toronto Press, 1997. Reprinted with permission of the publisher.

pp. 41, 68–67, 75–76, 96, 98, 100, 101, 121, 147, 148–49, 150–51, 152–53, 181, 183, 187: Quoted material reprinted by permission from J. Mueller (ed.) Katherine Parr – Complete Works and Correspondence, Chicago © 2011 by The University of Chicago. All rights reserved.

p. 106: Quoted material reprinted by permission from Springer Nature: Springer, Dordrecht, Dutch Anabaptism: Origin, Spread, Life and Thought (1450–1600) by C. Krahn © 1968

A catalogue record for this book is available from the British Library

Contents

Preface   vii

Part 1: Before

1. A Studious Young Lady   1

2. Of Daughters and Wives   11

3. The Great Ruffling   21

4. Conversion   34

5. Three Weddings and a Funeral   54

Part 2: The Crisis

6. Thunder Round the Throne   71

7. Divorce   82

8. The Year of Crisis   103

9. Condemned by the Law   121

10. Instant Desire   144

Part 3: After

11. Catherine and Anne in Historical Perspective   175

Bibliography   193

Index   195

Preface

This is the story of two remarkable women and the impact they had on the framing of England's religious identity at a crucial moment in history. In the summer of 1546 it was obvious to those close to the centre of power that the vastly overweight, sick and prematurely aged King Henry VIII was unlikely to live very much longer. No one could imagine what life would be like without the domineering presence of the man who had controlled and profoundly changed the nation for the last thirty-seven years. There were those who were wholeheartedly in favour of the Reformation – the severance of England's ties with Rome, the establishment of royal control over the national church, the propagation of evangelical teaching, the purging of all objects of Catholic "superstition" from the country's parish churches and the replacement of priest-controlled ritual by individual faith based on the study of the Bible. And there were those – the majority – who deplored all these innovations and hoped for a return to the "good old days" which would see the English church restored to papal obedience and the English state living in concord with its Catholic neighbours.

It was increasingly obvious that the Crown would pass to Prince Edward, Henry's son, who had not yet reached his ninth birthday. Given this uncertainty, councillors inevitably jostled for power and factions formed within the royal court. Everyone at the political centre wanted to have a hand in framing the policies which would be adopted in the new reign. At the same time, such manoeuvring could not be seen to be too obvious; even to mention the king's impending death was considered treason. Councillors and courtiers were walking on eggshells, desperate not to offend a king whose moods changed from day to day and whose constant pain from suppurating leg ulcers made him unpredictable and irascible.

We will be exploring in detail events which took place at the centre of Tudor politics during June and July 1546. They form a tense "in camera" drama involving a few characters, but they have a long pre-history involving several participants as far away from the political centre as Lincolnshire and a post-history which affected the entire nation. Heading the cast of *dramatis personae* are two extraordinary women. Catherine Parr was Henry VIII's last wife; a lady of considerable intellect and profound spirituality, she has the unique distinction of being the first English female author who deliberately published books under her own name. Anne Askew was the forthright daughter of a Midlands gentleman, who also wrote about her beliefs and her sufferings; she can never have imagined that her printed works would have the wide-reaching impact they achieved. The simple fact that both women have provided personal testimonies to their faith enables us to tell their interconnected story in more depth than would be possible if we were relying solely on official documents. It is a story at once sobering and stirring. Above all, it is an inspiring tale of religious faith pushed to the limits of endurance and the precipice of personal disaster.

PART 1

Before

Chapter 1

A Studious Young Lady

*M*ost of England's ancient buildings guard their secrets well. An unimposing squat, brick gatehouse standing alone in lush Lee Valley Park just outside Hoddesdon in Hertfordshire does not shout to passers-by, "Royal murder was planned here!" or "A Tudor queen lived in this place!" Yet, to students of Stuart history the Rye House Plot is familiar as an abortive attempt in 1683 to assassinate King Charles II and his brother, the Duke of York. Fewer people still will associate this very unregal site as the family home of the young Catherine Parr. Rye House was a modest dwelling even by the standards of the Tudor landed gentry.

Built in the mid-fifteenth century when the rivalry between the houses of Lancaster and York divided the country and sent armies in pursuit of each other across the shires, Rye House was situated within twenty miles of the key "Wars of the Roses" battles fought at Barnet and St Albans. Its prudent owner constructed a fortified manor house, surrounded by a wide moat and a stout wall; however, its living accommodation within these defensive boundaries was sufficient for only a comparatively small household. The buildings lay around three sides of a courtyard and consisted, on the ground floor, of a hall, a large parlour, a smaller parlour and domestic offices. The two floors above would have provided the sleeping chambers and the garrets for the servants. This quiet house, away from the busy world of the Tudor court and England's commercial metropolis, was, however, just off the road from London to Cambridge and so had easy access to important hubs of political and intellectual activity. This was essential for owners who needed access to the nation's government and who also wished to be considered among the English elite. Such a man was Sir Thomas Parr.

The family originated in Westmorland and, during the wars of the fifteenth century, had supported the Yorkist cause. However, William, Baron Parr of Kendal was more committed to the principle of legitimate monarchy than he was to the White Rose, and, when Richard III usurped the throne and disinherited the sons of his brother, Edward IV, Parr abandoned all involvement in national politics and lived his remaining days quietly. Soon after his death, his widow, Elizabeth Parr, married Sir Nicholas Vaux, a friend of Lady Margaret Beaufort, Henry VII's mother, thereby establishing good relations with the new Tudor regime. Elizabeth's son, Thomas, was still a child at this time but, in due course, he was introduced to the life of the court. His advancement seems to have begun around the turn of the century and the next glimpse we have of him is as Master of the Wards.

This is significant for at least three reasons. It shows that Thomas was high in the king's favour. It suggests that he gained his position via Lady Margaret who was a real power behind the throne, and it indicates that he had the talent and expertise to hold a position of extreme importance at the heart of Tudor power. Thomas Parr was well educated and well trained for the role he was destined to play in later life. Evidence is scanty but it is surmised that the young man studied at Oxford and was a member of the scholarly circle gathered around Lady Margaret. We also know that he was on friendly terms with Thomas More, who was also a distant relative. More was one of the leading intellectuals of the day and an advocate of the radical educational principles of the Renaissance. Parr was also influenced by his cousin, Cuthbert Tunstall, a lawyer and diplomat who rose to high office under the Tudors. All this was a promising start for a man entering royal service.

Henry VII was, to put it mildly, extremely careful with money. He was determined to put the Crown on a sound financial footing and personally supervised government accounts, which to an unprecedented extent became closely intermeshed with his own household accounts. Henry ruthlessly exploited all potential sources of royal income. This included prerogative income –

monies derived from the king's feudal rights as landholder in chief. One of the most lucrative of these was wardship. When a major landholder died leaving a minor as his heir all rights reverted to the Crown, which administered the property and received all rents and dues until the heir came of age. Understandably, families with considerable territorial assets often tried to conceal the inheritance of minors. Henry was determined to tighten his control of wardship and the new official, Master of the Wards, was provided with a sufficient staff to travel the country and ensure that the Exchequer was not being cheated out of feudal revenue. This office was very lucrative. Wardships were valuable commodities. For example, they carried the authority to arrange the marriage of wards, with the concomitant merging of estates. Therefore, there were always potential customers bidding to buy wardships. They were an important source of ready cash for the king – and for the Master of the Wards, who took a cut from all transactions.

It was in 1508, the last full year of Henry VII's reign, that Thomas married for the second time, his first wife having died. The new Mistress Parr was Maud Green, who came from another clan with court connections. Her family closet, however, was not without its skeletons. They were of ancient Yorkist stock, connected by marriage to the Woodvilles, Edward IV's in-laws, and had been members of the court. In 1506 Maud's father, Sir Thomas Green, was among a group of alleged Yorkist conspirators taken to the Tower. Though exonerated by a commission of inquiry, Sir Thomas died in captivity.

At the time of their marriage Thomas Parr was about twenty-five and his bride sixteen. They were firmly ensconced in the royal household and, in 1509, they were among those of his father's servants whom the new, athletic, fun-loving king chose to retain. Determined to make his court the most glittering in Christendom, Henry VIII soon made various additions to his entourage, including a resplendent body of personal guards – the Gentlemen Pensioners – to attend him on ceremonial occasions. Thomas Parr was created master of this body. He was also knighted and appointed High Sheriff of Northamptonshire (1509) and Lincolnshire (1510). Maud Parr was not overlooked in the handing out of honours. One of Henry's first decisions was to marry his dead brother's widow, Catherine of Aragon. An enhanced entourage had to be created for the new queen, and Maud became a lady-in-waiting.

Those early days of the new reign were exciting for the courtier couple. The queen reported to her father, "Our time is spent in continual festival." There were banquets and tourneys and disguisings and hunting parties. Henry spent liberally on his own pleasures and on rewards for his companions. As the court moved around the various royal residences within easy reach of the capital, life was very different from what it had been in the days of the old, parsimonious king. The Parrs had their own properties where they stayed when their duties did not demand attendance on their majesties. As well as estates in the North and Midlands, which were augmented by inheritances from deceased relatives on both sides of the family, the couple owned a town house in the fashionable district of Blackfriars and the easily accessible rural bolthole of Rye House.

Clouds, however, occasionally drifted across the Tudor sky. On New Year's Day 1511, Queen Catherine brought a boy child into the world. Henry was ecstatic. He rushed off to the shrine of Our Lady of Walsingham to give thanks, then returned to host lavish celebrations at court. Seven weeks later the young prince was dead. The disappointment and humiliation weighed heavily with the king. He certainly never went on pilgrimage again. It must have been about this time that the Parrs suffered the same sorrow. Their firstborn son also died soon after birth. This may have created a special bond between Maud and the queen, for they became and remained very close. When, a year later, a baby girl appeared in the Parr household she was named Catherine, after the queen. Two more children were added to the family, a son, William (c.1513), and a daughter, Anne (c.1515).

It is pleasant to imagine the young family of Thomas and Maud in the quiet country retreat of Rye House, where they certainly must have spent some of their days in the care of nurses and a tutor while their parents were engaged in court duties. Catherine was one of the first girls in England to receive the benefit of a humanist education (that is, a learning programme based on a fresh understanding of Greek and Latin writers that emphasized the importance of the full realization of human potential). The world in which she and her siblings grew up was changing as Renaissance influences penetrated England. Old customs and values were being challenged by an intellectual avant-garde rediscovering classical literature and philosophy and new ideas reaching northern Europe via Italy. One traditional conviction called in question was the appropriate education of women. Since the 1480s one of the major topics for debate in humanist circles had been the relationship of the sexes. For example in a brief Latin treatise of 1501, Mario Equicola, a scholar in the service of the d' Este family of Ferrara, complained:

> … woman is occupied exclusively at home where she grows feeble from leisure, she is not permitted to occupy her mind with anything other than needle and thread.[1]

Equicola was not alone in urging that since men and women were alike in both being created with immortal souls their minds should be equally open to stimulus. The leading scholar of the day, Desiderius Erasmus, was also very scornful of traditional attitudes towards women. This Dutch doyen of the international humanist community paid several visits to England in the early years of the century, was warmly welcomed by Thomas More, Cuthbert Tunstall, and their circle and taught for a while at Cambridge. He once wrote a witty satire for Margaret More, Thomas's daughter, which poked fun at closed-minded conservatives. It took the form of a dialogue between Antronius, a monk, and Magdalia, a cultured lady:

> A: Distaff and spindle are the proper equipment for women.

> M: Isn't it a wife's business to manage the household and rear the children?

---

1 Cited in Rabil A. (ed.) *Henricus Cornelius Agrippa – Declaration on the Nobility and Pre-eminence of the Female Sex*, Chicago, 1996, p. 24.

A: It is.

M: Do you think she can manage so big a job without wisdom?

A: I suppose not.

M: But books teach me wisdom.

A: … I could put up with books, but not Latin ones.

M: Why not?

A: Because that language isn't for women.

M: Is it fitting for a German woman to learn French?

A: Of course.

M: Why?

A: To talk with those who know French.

M: And you think it unsuitable for me to know Latin in order to converse daily with authors so numerous, so eloquent, so learned, so wise …?

A: Books ruin women's wits – which are none too plentiful anyway.[2]

But Erasmus's biggest challenge to the religious establishment came in 1516 when he published his *Novum Instrumentum*, a new Latin translation of the New Testament based on the best available early Greek texts. It differed in some respects from the

---

2   Thompson C. (trans.) *Collected Works of Erasmus – Colloquies*, Toronto/Buffalo/London, 1997, pp. 502–3.

Vulgate of St Jerome, which had been the only approved version in the western church for over twelve centuries and the basis for all doctrine. What Erasmus was doing was suggesting that the Catholic Church could, theoretically, be in error. He went further: he suggested that the Bible was not the exclusive possession of clergy and scholars. It should be available to every Christian who could read – in the vernacular.

Another frequent visitor to England and friend of the avant garde intelligentsia was Juan Luis Vives. This Spanish scholar spent most of his life in the Netherlands where he came under the influence of Erasmus. In 1527 he wrote a detailed dissertation entitled *The Instruction of a Christian Woman* in which he recommended that high-born girls should share the intellectual training of their brothers, which included studying Latin, Greek, and philosophy. He enjoyed the favour of the king and queen and was appointed as a tutor to their only surviving child, Princess Mary.

Although we have little detailed information about the upbringing of the young Parrs we can locate it against this background of new thinking which was the height of fashion at the Tudor court. Catherine and Anne were, as Vives recommended, instructed by the same tutor as their brother. They learned to be fluent in Latin, French, and Italian, were taught mathematics and basic medicine. Tunstall (who became Bishop of London in 1522), as a close friend of the family, seems to have kept a watching brief on the development of the children. This continued after 1517, the year in which tragedy struck the little household. Sir Thomas Parr died suddenly, one of the first victims of a new, terrifying disease to reach England – the "sweating sickness". This influenza-like virus struck hard and fast. In crowded urban centres it carried off between a third and a half of the population. One of the places worse affected was the royal court. Henry VIII fled the capital at the first sign of infection, restricted access to his royal person, and kept on moving from residence to residence. The deaths among household personnel and councillors left serious holes in the fabric of government. It may have been the dislocation caused by the disease which partly explains what Maud Parr did next – or, rather, what she did not do.

The conventional course of action for Maud would have been to remarry. At twenty-five she was eminently eligible. There must have been several suitors attracted by the prospect of the widow's property and the control of the wardship of her children. Yet she remained unwed. Perhaps for several months during that terrible year the forging of marriage alliances did not figure prominently on the agenda of ambitious courtiers. Or perhaps Sir Thomas's relatives were anxious not to see his property passing under the control of some rival clan. Certainly, no one was more knowledgable about how to maintain her children's inheritance intact than the widow of the late Master of the Wards. Then, of course, there was Maud's standing in the queen's entourage. If she obtained Catherine of Aragon's support she might well be able to do what she wanted. And what she wanted was to remain single. Her brother-in-law, Sir William Parr, helped to fill part of the gap created by the death of her husband and seems to have been well liked by his nephew and nieces. Thus, for a few years, the course of the children's lives remained largely unchanged. The same was certainly not true of the wider world. Only days before Sir Thomas's death, a monk at Wittenberg in Saxony had raised a series of objections about papal claims to be able to influence the destiny of souls in purgatory. His name was Martin Luther. The Reformation had begun.

Maud had more immediate concerns. She had three children to set on their paths through life. That meant arranging advantageous marriages or establishing them at the royal court. In 1525 eleven-year-old William was placed in the household of Henry VIII's illegitimate son, the Duke of Richmond. Negotiations to find a husband for Catherine began at about the same time. They bore fruit in 1529, when a deal was struck with Sir Thomas Borough of Old Hall, Gainsborough, Lincolnshire, to pair Catherine with his son Edward; a rather sickly man some seven years her senior. Thus, at the age of sixteen, Catherine left her familiar homes in London and Hertfordshire for the very impressive fifteenth-century house on the edge of the fens which can still be seen. The Boroughs were the leading "upper gentry" family in the area and, in 1483, had entertained Richard of Gloucester on his way south to grab the crown from his young nephew. Sophisticated denizens of the

Tudor court looked on the leaders of Lincolnshire society with disdain. One such reported that he had never seen anywhere,

> Such a sight of asses, so unlike gentlemen as the most part of them be … Knights and esquires are meeter to be baileys [bailiffs]; men voiced good fashion, and, in truth, of wit, except in matters concerning their trade, which is to get goods only.[3]

Such a generalization was bordering on libellous, as we shall see, but Catherine will have found the company in the Borough household less than stimulating after the intellectual circles she had belonged to previously. However, we should not exaggerate; her new environment is unlikely to have come as a complete shock to her. The family had property in the area and she may well have visited the Parr manor of Maltby, some nineteen miles east of Gainsborough.

After a few months the young couple moved to a home of their own, deeper in the fenland at Kirton in Lindsey, in the north of the county. Here we encounter one of the tantalizing unknowns in our story. Kirton lies only nine miles from South Kelsey, where the lord of the manor was Sir William Ayscough (or Askew, to use the spelling which became more common), one of whose children was a ten-year-old daughter, christened Anne. It is inconceivable that the neighbouring gentlemen and their families were not acquainted and that, therefore, Catherine and Anne, whose destinies were to be so closely bound up together, did not know each other.

Unfortunately fate permitted Catherine little time or inclination for socializing during her brief stay in Lincolnshire. Caring for her frail husband must have kept her well occupied. Then, in the closing days of 1531 the news came that her mother had died. She could look for little comfort from her in-laws since she showed no sign of fulfilling her first duty to the Boroughs, that of providing an

---

3   John Williams to Thomas Cromwell, 27 October 1536, Gairdner J. (ed.), *Letters and Papers, Foreign and Domestic, Henry VIII*, London, 1888, Volume XI, p. 888. All further references take the form *L & P*.

heir to their estates. Perhaps it came as something of a relief when Edward gave up his struggle against declining health in April 1533. She could now take some control of her own life. She turned to her relatives and, after some fifteen months of widowhood, a second marriage was negotiated. Her new husband was John Neville, Baron Latimer, a second cousin of her father. The arrangement was eminently suitable for both parties. Forty-year-old Neville had been twice widowed and had a son and daughter, aged fourteen and ten respectively. They, and especially Margaret Neville, needed a mother and the baron hoped for more children. Catherine craved the security this new union would bring, particularly as it renewed her connections with the royal court. Neville had earlier been a member of the king's guard and had served on military campaigns in France. As a member of the Council of the North he was now one of the magnates trusted by Henry VIII with control of affairs in the turbulent border counties. From his ancestral home, Snape Castle, North Yorkshire, just off the Great North Road near Bedale, he stood ready to counter frequent Scottish incursions, as well as maintain Crown control of the powerful magnates who were sufficiently far from the capital to enjoy a large measure of independence. Catherine settled to enjoy the comfort of her new home. But, after a little more than two years, disaster struck.

CHAPTER 2

Of Daughters and Wives

The Askews of Lincolnshire and Nottinghamshire originated farther north, beyond the Humber. Some of their extensive lands lay near to the Latimer stronghold of Snape Castle; indeed, the family name still survives in the township of Aiskew, close by Bedale. But they were more than Yorkshire squires. They had long been prominent in national life. One ancestor, Bishop William Ayscough (1395–1450) (as the name was then spelled), had the unfortunate distinction of being murdered in Jack Cade's rebellion by a mob angered at his presiding at the marriage of Henry VI and Margaret of Anjou. At this time another Sir William Askew (1422–56) was Chief Justice of the Common Pleas. Throughout the troubled fifteenth century the family remained staunch supporters of the Lancastrian cause and their fortunes fluctuated accordingly. It was Sir William's son, John, who relocated into Lincolnshire. By dint of an advantageous marriage, he acquired property south of the river and moved his principal residence to Stallingborough, near Grimsby, which was then a major coastal port. John (d.1491) lived long enough to see the final Lancastrian triumph under the leadership of Henry Tudor, and his son, another William, was present at the Battle of Stoke in 1487 when the last serious Yorkist challenge led by John de la Pole was defeated. The Askews were now well ensconced in royal favour and, in 1501, William received a signal mark of royal favour.

> This year was sent into England the King of Spain's third daughter, named Catherine, to be married to the Prince Arthur, and she landed at Plymouth the eighth day of

October, and was received into London in the most royal wise the twelfth day of November, then Friday. And the Sunday following she was married at St Paul's church ... And the feast was held in the Bishop of London's palace. And the day of her receiving into London were made many rich pageants; first at the bridge, at the conduit in Gracechurch Street, the conduit in Cornhill, the standard in Cheapside (the cross newly gilded), at the little conduit; and at St Paul's west door there was running wine – red claret and white – all the day of the marriage. And at the same marriage the king made fifty-seven knights.[4]

Among the fifty-seven gentlemen to be thus honoured in the midst of the rejoicing at the ill-fated marriage of Henry VII's elder son to Catherine of Aragon was William Askew of Stallingborough.

Sir William eventually retired to concentrate on managing his Lincolnshire estates, but not before he had secured a firm place for his heir, William (1486–1540), in the Tudor court. He was attached to the household of Prince Henry, a boy not much younger than himself. This William married Elizabeth, daughter of another wealthy courtier, William Wrottesley of Reading. He established his country residence at Nuthall, Nottinghamshire (now part of suburban Nottingham), which was more convenient for a man with important duties at the royal court. It was, therefore, at Nuthall that his five surviving children were born. He retained this as his principal residence even after his father died in 1509, leaving him extensive lands across the East Midlands.

He needed all the income his property provided. Keeping up appearances in the court of the new, extrovert, spendthrift King Henry VIII was an expensive business. Even more costly was accompanying Henry on his military escapade in France in 1513. William was appointed to raise and equip a body of Lincolnshire levies for this grandiloquent venture. To pay for this privilege he had to part with "the manor of Nethertointon and lands in

---

4 *Grey Friars' Chronicle*, Camden Society, Old Series, 1852, p. 27.

Saucethorpe, Tangton and Hagworthingham".[5] However, he was rewarded for all his time, trouble and expense. After the fall of the small French town of Therouanne, Henry distributed honours to his captains. William Askew was among those who were knighted.

During the ensuing years Sir William was much at court. In 1520 he was chosen (as was Sir Thomas Borough, Catherine Parr's future father-in-law) to attend the king on his next cross-Channel foray, the diplomatic extravaganza known as the Field of the Cloth of Gold. As he set out that spring, he left behind his wife, Elizabeth, and five children – Francis, Martha, Christopher, Edward, and a newly born girl, christened Anne. Thereafter we find Askew mentioned again in other major events. When, in May 1522, the Emperor Charles V paid a visit to England, Sir William was in the royal entourage that went with King Henry to greet the Habsburg at Canterbury. During the following weeks he was with the court at Westminster, Greenwich, Richmond, Hampton Court, Windsor, and Winchester where he helped to organize the sumptuous royal entertainments which systematically destocked each of the manors at which the court stayed.

Back in the Midlands all was not well. Nottinghamshire and Lincolnshire were among the counties which succumbed to a virulent outbreak of sweating sickness. In 1521 Elizabeth Askew died. Another fatality among Askew's friends in the shire was Sir William Hansard of South Kelsey. He died in January 1522. But death had not finished with his family. In April, his only son and heir also fell victim to the disease. He left a widowed mother, two sisters, his own widowed wife, and a baby daughter (who was now the heiress to all the Hansard lands).

The fate of the Hansards would now be decided by the current Master of the Wards. That was none other than Cardinal Wolsey, who had appropriated this lucrative office for himself. As in most such cases, the wardship of little Elizabeth Hansard would go to the highest bidder and there were several interested parties. Askew moved swiftly and adroitly. Not only did he, with

---

5   Brewster H. C. *South Kelsey Notes*, MS in Lincoln Cathedral Library, 1898, p. 54.

the help of friends at court, acquire the wardship of Elizabeth, he also married Elizabeth's recently widowed grandmother (also called Elizabeth). This gave him control of all the Hansard estates and it also provided the opportunity for the arrangement to be perpetuated, for it was understood that when the heiress came of marriageable age she would become the wife of Sir William's eldest son, Francis. Having brought off this legal coup the new master of South Kelsey set about consolidating all his territorial holdings. In a series of deals with his neighbours and land agents he made himself one of the wealthiest gentlemen in a wide area of eastern England; he had residences at Stallingborough, South Kelsey, Nuthall, Basing and Spalding, and land in Lincolnshire, Nottinghamshire, Leicestershire, and Yorkshire. He also acted as steward for Thornton and Selby Abbeys and Nun Cotham Priory, services which brought him in £6.35 per year (approximately £35,000 in modern terms).

It was about this time that Francis Askew, aged thirteen or fourteen, was sent to Cambridge, to gain the intellectual grounding, particularly in the law, that was considered essential for those destined to play an important part in managing estates and in English local government. Did the boy's father realize that the fenland university was fast becoming one of the hotspots of religious radicalism? In 1511–13 Erasmus had lectured there, bringing the exciting new thinking of Renaissance humanism and introducing the study of Greek to the curriculum. But the event that was destined to revolutionize English society far more than anyone could possibly have foreseen occurred 550 miles away in Saxony, when in the autumn of 1517 Martin Luther, an Augustinian friar, challenged official Catholic teaching about purgatory, penance, and the authority of the pope.

One of the more astonishing facts about the Reformation is the speed at which it spread. Within two years of Luther's "95 Theses" (theological debating points) being issued, Erasmus could write to inform the Wittenberg monk that his writings were being admired in England by some "very great people". In 1520 the son of a Shropshire gentleman, in London for his education, could write home to his father, "Sir, as for news, there is none, but of late there was heretics here, which do take Luther's opinions".[6] In May of the following year Cardinal Wolsey personally presided over a spectacular bonfire of heretical books in St Paul's churchyard. The authorities were obviously seriously alarmed by the spate of books entering the country from German and Dutch printing presses.

The only explanation for this intellectual and spiritual upheaval was that Luther was voicing an idea whose time had come. Paradoxically, it was a shock and yet also expected. Criticism of the religious establishment had been growing for decades. Now reformers were challenging the doctrinal foundation underpinning the establishment. Furthermore, they were doing so with the support of an authority older than the papacy – the written word of God. Now that books were printed and not laboriously handwritten in monastic scriptoria the literate and curious were able to lay their hands on Luther's treatise *On Good Works* which set forth a belief in the necessity of faith alone for salvation, the supreme importance of the Bible, and the freedom of the Christian soul from all ecclesiastical laws and sanctions. They were able to read *The Address to the Christian Nobility of the German Nation*, which exhorted all princes to rule fully in their realms and throw off the shackles of papal control. They might pore over *The Freedom of the Christian Man* in which Luther further expounded his conviction that no pope, bishop or priest could stand between the believer and his God (a conviction which he dramatically illustrated by publicly burning copies of the canon law in 1520). But most forthright and inflammatory of all the secretly read and carefully guarded Lutheran scripts was *The Babylonian Captivity of the Church*, which was nothing less than a devastating attack on the entire sacramental system of the Roman Church; it overthrew transubstantiation;[7]

---

6   Historical Manuscripts Commission, *The Manuscripts of Shrewsbury and Coventry Corporations [Etc] Fourth Report, Appendix: Part X*, London, 1899, p. 48.

7   Transubstantiation was the philosophical explanation of how, at the mass, bread and wine were changed by the priest into the body and blood of Christ. It claimed that, though the "accidents" (the outward

drastically altered the nature of penance; denied completely the sacramental understanding of ordination, confirmation, and marriage; and denounced the monastic life as worthless in the eyes of God.

Luther's writings were soon followed by those of the more extreme Swiss reformer, Huldrych Zwingli. They added similar fuel to the same fires. His *On Divine and Human Justice* explored the relationship between church and state, stressing the need for complete harmony between them but confining church leaders to the possession of spiritual authority alone. The basis of Christian faith as a personal relationship between the Christian and his Saviour was set forth in *On True and False Religion*, which called for no other kind of mediator, such as a priest.

The most significant feature about the spread of new ideas in England was the change in the sociological composition of native heresy. Heretofore, religious unorthodoxy had been associated with the "ignorant" peasant and artisan classes. Now it was reaching and influencing the upper strata. As we have seen, Renaissance humanism was in fashion and new educational principles were in vogue. Questioning orthodoxy was becoming respectable. Nowhere was this truer than in the royal court. Henry VIII considered himself an enlightened "modern" ruler who patronized the leading thinkers of the day and enjoyed the company of men au fait with the latest ideas. Sir William Askew would have experienced this invigorating, self-conscious, intellectual libertarianism. It is safe to assume that it influenced the way he brought up his children. He now had three sons (Francis, Christopher, and Edward), three daughters (Martha, Anne, and Jane) and a step-daughter (Elizabeth Hansard). It is more than likely that he responded to the new trend of educating them all together by hiring a tutor. What is clear is that the girls were taught to read and write and to have a basic grasp of Latin. More importantly, they became familiar with the New Testament in English, for a translation by William Tyndale

---

appearance) of the elements remained, their "substance" (their essential essence or character) had been transformed.

was making its way into England from foreign presses by 1526.[8]

Evangelical "heresy", therefore, reached the South Kelsey household via three routes: Sir William told his family what everyone was talking about at court; colporteurs came to the door hawking books smuggled into England, concealed in barrels and bales, via the east coast ports (including Stallingborough); and Francis reported on the brash novelties exciting his university friends.

At this very time, Cambridge was the religious nursery of men who would become the leading movers and shakers of the English Reformation. As early as 1521 there may have been a group of senior academics meeting at the White Horse Inn to discuss the ideas of Erasmus, Luther, and other radicals. Those not in sympathy with them dubbed the tavern "Little Germany". Among those congregating there were several who would be household names within a few years – Thomas Cranmer, Hugh Latimer, Miles Coverdale, Robert Barnes, Thomas Bilney. These freethinkers were, apparently, undeterred by the vigilance of the authorities. In 1521 a bonfire of Luther's books was made in front of the university church. It would be fascinating to know whether Francis Askew was somewhere in the crowd of onlookers; if so, he might well have recalled the blaze, destined to herald a sequence of other fires in which the victims would not be printed paper, but flesh and bones.

Of the five named above, four would perish as martyrs. The first to go to the stake must have been known to young Askew. Thomas Bilney ("Little Bilney" as he was affectionately known) was one of many academics who rethought his faith as a result of reading Erasmus's New Testament. Not only did his understanding of the Gospel change; he also realized the importance of putting his beliefs into action. He spent much time visiting the sick in the lazar house and the inmates of the stinking prison. His practical Christianity made a great impression on members of the White Horse Inn "holy club" and, doubtless, on others also. Had he influenced just one man, Hugh Latimer, he would have earned his place in the story of the Reformation, for Latimer went on to

8   See p. 36.

become one of the most popular and effective preachers of the age. Bilney was no mean proclaimer himself and, in the mid-1520s he gave himself to extensive preaching tours of East Anglia. His troublesome zeal could not go unnoticed and Cuthbert Tunstall (Bishop of London since 1522) had him arrested. After many long sessions of interrogation, Bilney recanted and, after a spell in prison, was released. But he was a broken man, distressed not by his sufferings, but by his own weakness in denying what he believed was the truth. He resumed his evangelical preaching, knowing what the result of this must be. In August 1531 this gentle and much-loved advocate of the "New Learning" was burned to death at Norwich.

Robert Barnes, a considerable scholar, took his doctorate in divinity in 1523 but was soon teaching doctrines alien to the curriculum of the schools. The first of his many investigations was before the vice-chancellor in 1525. It is reported that the proceedings were interrupted by noisy student demonstrations. Like most rebels, Barnes and other advocates of change readily won a following among the young. It was this generation of educated young men of Francis Askew's acquaintance who would become the leaders of English society in the 1530s and 1540s. As for Barnes, he weathered the changing winds of the early Reformation before going to the fire in Smithfield in 1540. The inspiration of "heroes" like Bilney and Barnes goes a long way towards explaining how the New Learning won over large numbers of the ruling classes.

A further factor influencing the spread of the Reformation among the nation's elite was, of course, the modified support given it by the king. One of the most pregnant coincidences in English history was that the spread of revolutionary ideas occurred at the very time that Henry VIII fell out with the papacy. From 1527 he became increasingly desperate for the annulment of his marriage, something the pope declined to provide. The conflict escalated until, by 1540, much of medieval Catholicism had been dismantled.

In the relative peace and quiet of South Kelsey the Askew children were growing up and Sir William had to make plans for their advancement. It was the norm for sons of the nobility and gentry to be farmed out to other households where they would learn the graces of civilized behaviour and also make "useful" contacts. In placing Edward, Sir William had a stroke of luck. There was a lesser gentry family whose principal seat was at Aslockton in Nottinghamshire, not twelve miles from the Askew manor at Nuthall. They probably did not feature prominently among Sir William's friends and acquaintances but, in 1531, all that changed. One member of that family, already known to Francis from his student days, was rocketed from rural obscurity to the very centre of national life. His name was Thomas Cranmer. He had been brought to the attention of the king as one who might be able to find a way out of the impasse of Henry's relations with the pope. Rapidly, the bewildered Cranmer found himself employed on ambassadorial missions, taken into the king's confidence, showered with honours and finally appointed Primate of all England. He was destined to become the first Archbishop of Canterbury in the independent Church of England. Under these circumstances, Askew decided that no one could be better qualified to take charge of his second son. Accordingly, Edward became a page in the household of Thomas Cranmer and the Askews forged another link with the reform movement. Now, young Christopher's feet had to be placed on the ladder leading to wealth and rank. This was achieved with even more spectacular success. We do not know with whom Christopher first saw service, but he progressed quickly and by 1536 had gained a much-coveted position as Gentleman of the King's Privy Chamber.

On their visits home from Cambridge, Lambeth, and the peripatetic court, Sir William's sons must have arrived full of news of the progress of religious change. Francis could report that students were encouraged to read the Bible for themselves. Scholastic glosses and traditional interpretations of Scripture were thrown overboard. Degrees and lectures in canon law were abolished. Edward had stories to tell of his master's deliberate encouragement of heretics, his appointment of some to ecclesiastical office and angry visits to the archbishop by outraged orthodox churchmen. The gossip from court would be of the rise to power of the upstart Thomas Cromwell, of replacing the upstart Wolsey, of the triumph of Anne Boleyn and her patron the Duke of Norfolk, and of the encouragement given by the queen's faction to the new ideas. Above all, Christopher was able to bring home details of the king's breach with Rome. The pace of change was accelerating alarmingly. Observing the swelling river of anti-clerical, anti-papal criticism, Thomas Cromwell turned its energy into the formulation of a mass of legislation passed by the "Reformation Parliament" (1529–36). This culminated in his masterstroke – the Act of Supremacy – which finally cut the Gordian knot of Anglo-papal relations, by establishing that the King of England was head of the church within his realm.

For the time being, the even tenor of life at South Kelsey Hall was undisturbed (though far from uninfluenced) by these events. Sir William Askew and his family enjoyed years of peace and prosperity. Like other landowner families, they prospered from the fallout of the Reformation. But not before they had all faced a major crisis.

CHAPTER 3

The Great Ruffling

The chain reaction of the English Reformation began as a simple issue of canon law: Henry VIII asserted that his marriage to his brother's widow was a violation of holy Scripture and, therefore, void. All that was required was that Pope Clement VII should, for the appropriate fee, formally annul Henry's union with Catherine of Aragon and that Catherine should meekly accept the fait accompli. But, for various political reasons, his holiness could not and, for reasons of conscience, the queen would not comply with the king's wishes. Neither side would give way. Each sought support at home and abroad in a dispute which became increasingly bitter as year succeeded year. It was a dispute that divided the nation.

In many ways it would be truer to say that it provided the emotional focus for divisions that already existed and, in so doing, accelerated the spread of discord. The Act of Supremacy (1534) gave the force of law to Henry's claim to headship of the English church and provided severe penalties (including death in the most extreme cases) for any who persisted in asserting the authority of the "Bishop of Rome". Actions such as the beheading of Thomas More, Henry's erstwhile friend and councillor (1535), indicated just how serious the king was in making use of the statutes embodying the seismic shift in English religious life. Matters could have rested there had not responsibility for enforcing change been entrusted to a man committed to evangelical reform.

In 1534, Thomas Cromwell was made Vice-Gerent in Spirituals with authority to carry out visitations of all religious establishments. He went much further: he made a determined assault on public opinion. His detailed administrative and publicity campaign can only be described as astonishing. It had two aspects – positive and negative. By means of sponsoring preachers, writers and artists, he ensured a continuous output of evangelical propaganda. At the same time he removed many of the symbols of the old faith that exercised a silent but powerful influence over people's minds. Shrines and pilgrimage centres were destroyed. Public bonfires were made of images that had been venerated for generations.

The super-efficient Cromwell lost no time in preparing for his ecclesiastical asset-stripping. His first step was a thorough stocktaking of the English church. Between January and September 1535, royal commissioners roamed every diocese demanding complete accounts of parish incomes and possessions from the priests and churchwardens. The object of this *Valor Ecclesiasticus* was the accurate assessment of the church's wealth so that it might be fully and accurately taxed by the government. The unfortunate commissioners charged with this snooping were, for the most part, the leading local gentry. Much of the unpopularity of royal policy rubbed off on to them. The knights and gentlemen of the shires thus found a wedge being driven between them and their people. For many who had a sneaking dislike for the new royal policies, there was also the additional discomfort of a troubled conscience. But the *Valor Ecclesiasticus* was only the beginning. Before all the reports were in, a second visitation had been set afoot. In July, specially chosen clerical and lay agents were touring the monastic houses of the realm, enquiring into their spiritual condition – and their wealth.

In market place, church, and tavern, men speculated together as to what these investigations might mean. Speculation begat bewilderment and wild rumour: taxes on church property were to be increased; shrines were about to be despoiled of their jewels and precious metals; royal officers were coming to seize reliquaries, holy statues, and the traditional objects of devotion; the very parish churches themselves were in danger as the king was going to grasp all the land of the monasteries and cast the religious adrift in the world. Such rumours bred an atmosphere of tense resentment. Many, perhaps most, people could not credit that all

England's religious houses were in danger, but those in the know realized the political significance of such a policy. The monasteries were the principal bastions of papal support, potential focal points of challenge to the government's proceedings. They had to go. But there was another very tempting reason for the biggest land grab in English history. The vast acreage passing into government hands was destined to pass out of government hands – sold on to acquisitive aristocratic and gentry landowners. In other words the church's wealth would be used to buy support for the dismantling of the church's power.

In March 1536, the attack on English monasticism began in earnest. An Act was passed for the closure of all houses with an annual income of less than £200 per year. Within weeks, Cromwell set in train yet another commission. The lawyers and local gentry appointed as commissioners for each county were to make a fresh, more accurate, valuation of the property of the doomed houses. Furthermore, they were to quiz all superiors about the spiritual condition of their brethren: Are there any who wish to forsake the religious life altogether? Would any be prepared to take a benefice as a secular clergyman? Would those maintaining their vows mind being moved to another house of the order? The gentry approached their inquisitorial task with mixed feelings. Many were friends of their cloistered neighbours and valued the prayers offered daily for their ancestors. However, ex-monastic land coming onto the market would provide a once-in-a-lifetime opportunity to extend and consolidate their property holdings. Of one fact the commissioners were in no doubt: they would be received with resentment and hostility.

On 3 October 1536, Sir William Askew set out from South Kelsey to ride to Caistor where he was to meet his colleagues for the next round of their investigation. The nine commissioners (including Lord Borough) were confronted by an assembly of several thousand angry men who had come from a wide area of the fenland to resist the royal initiative. The Lincolnshire Rebellion had begun. Some of the gentlemen escaped but Askew was among the commissioners arrested and eventually carried off to Lincoln, where they were kept under guard in the cathedral close. Many more bands of protesters converged on the city and went on a looting spree. It was an extremely confused situation – confused and frightening. What made matters worse for Sir William was the arrival of his sons, Francis and Edward. Rebels had ridden over to South Kelsey and taken the boys hostage, leaving the ladies of the household terrified.

What the protesters wanted was for the gentlemen to take on the leadership of the rebellion and present to the government their demands for a reversal of religious policy and the adoption of certain social reforms. But there were differences among the leaders about what they were asking for and how best to proceed. The more extreme dissidents were all for murdering their captives – to show how determined they were.

Meanwhile, news had reached London, where Henry made plans to suppress the uprising. Naturally, he despatched to the troubled area members of his own entourage who had local knowledge. Young Christopher Askew of the Privy Chamber was among those sent to Lincoln. But Sir William's son did not dare to venture further than Spalding for fear of being captured. From there he sent back to Cromwell a gloomy mix of fact and rumour, some of it gruesome. He assessed the insurgents as being everywhere in power and venting their spleen on Cromwell's agents. They had, he claimed, hanged one of the minister's men and baited another to death with dogs, having covered the poor man with a bull's skin. Christopher was particularly anguished to hear that his father and brothers were all held by the rebels.[9]

The king sent messages to leaders in the shires to muster their retainers and tenants and rendezvous at Ampthill in Bedfordshire with the Duke of Suffolk, who was placed in charge of the royal army. By 9 October this army was on the move. The news stirred mixed feelings among the captive gentlemen. They were pleased to know that relief was on its way but anxious about how the king would react to their handling of the crisis. They had early concluded that their only course of action was delaying tactics and had held frequent meetings with the rebel leaders about how

---

9   *L & P*, XI, 567.

best to present their complaints to the king. But the patience of their captors was wearing thin. Askew and his colleagues found themselves between a rock and a hard place. If the ringleaders of the revolt suspected that they were prevaricating, they might drag them out for summary execution as enemies of the people. If Henry suspected that the gentlemen had really joined the rebels he might order their execution as enemies of the Crown.

In fact, they only narrowly escaped the former fate. After an angry meeting in the cathedral on 10 October, a small group of hotheads decided to attack the gentlemen as they left by the west door. Fortunately, someone overheard their plans and revealed them to the proposed victims, who slipped out by a side door. Their tactics (the only ones they could have adopted) paid off. The rapid approach of well-armed troops was enough to discourage the rebels, who now began to drift away to their homes. By 13 October, when Suffolk rode into Lincoln, the gentlemen were more than ready to make their formal submission.

But this was very far from being the end of the crisis. The Lincolnshire uprising had alarmed the king and his ministers. What followed came close to bringing down the regime. When the royal army clattered through the streets of Lincoln they were met by sullen crowds. Suffolk reported that scarce a man raised his cap to the king's general. This resentment was shared by many in the lands beyond Humber but the dissident movement in the North differed from that of Lincolnshire in two important respects: it embraced all classes and it was well led. The major landowners of the northern shires had a long tradition of semi-independence from central government and there were men of standing ready to do what Askew and others would not – put themselves at the head of a popular reactionary movement. That movement provided itself with a banner, proclaiming its religious nature – the five wounds of Christ – and it claimed an identity more exalted than that of mere political protest – the Pilgrimage of Grace.

The man who assumed leadership of the movement was Robert Aske, a lawyer from an old Richmondshire family. He correctly assessed the failure in Lincolnshire as the result of poor leadership and unclear objectives. He easily raised a force of 9,000 men and, on 16 October, seized control of York. Spontaneous uprisings occurred in several other places and, within a week, 30,000 armed "pilgrims" had congregated at Doncaster. This was the pivotal moment of Henry VIII's reign. On the outcome would depend the relationship between Crown and nobility, the relationship between church and state, the relationship between England and Rome, the fate of English monasticism, the progress of religious reform and, if the uprising got really out of hand, the future of the Tudor dynasty. It was little wonder that Henry moved himself and his court into Windsor Castle and despatched more troops to the North. Two separate detachments made their way to the troubled area. The Duke of Norfolk set out with 5,000 men, while the Earl of Shrewsbury mustered 7,000 in the Midlands. They were hopelessly outnumbered by the rebel host, which was growing daily. Since the "pilgrims" were also well led they were unlikely to be overawed by the approach of the king's army.

The traditional leaders in the North found themselves in the same dilemma as that which had faced the Lincolnshire squirearchy. Their social position and, in some cases, their religious convictions inclined them to join the movement. Their responsibility as representatives of law and order obliged them to suppress it. To simply run away would mean leaving their homes and families unguarded. Their only option was to take control of the Pilgrimage and hope to buy time. This would certainly leave them with some difficult explaining to do if the rebellion proved unsuccessful. Henry, who well understood the divided loyalties of the northern magnates, would not flinch from making examples of prominent "traitors". Yet, if they lost the confidence of the rebels, their end might be equally bloody.

On 14 or 15 October, Baron Latimer was forced by his own tenants to swear the rebels' oath and lead them to rendezvous with the main host at York. From there the multitude marched for a gathering in force at Pontefract, where Archbishop Edward Lee and several local magnates had taken refuge in the castle. They arrived on 22 October to discover that Lord Darcy had embraced the military leadership of the rebellion and that, with Robert Aske and others, he was planning nothing less than a march to London.

Norfolk, meanwhile, had reported to the king that a military contest was out of the question. He knew that the only hope of regaining control was diplomacy – if necessary duplicitous diplomacy. Henry, for all the angry statements he directed at the pilgrims, probably agreed. If the rebels could be kept talking, their own internal divisions and the onset of winter might produce the same result as in Lincolnshire. However, that possibility had also occurred to the demonstrators; they were determined not to abandon their position of strength. Two weeks of frenzied debate followed at the end of which the pilgrims presented their coherent list of demands. These included a reversal of religious policy, surrender of the king's "evil councillors" and the calling of a parliament to meet in Nottingham or York. Latimer was a member of the delegation which set out to meet with Norfolk at Doncaster to hear the king's response.

What the rebels heard was music to their ears: his majesty had graciously considered their grievances and would take them seriously. He would summon the parliament they had requested. Moreover, he would grant full and free pardon for their actions if they would now disperse. Was Henry the originator of these concessions or was it Norfolk who provided "the gentle answer that turneth away wrath"? Whoever was responsible for the duplicity, it worked. Though several of the Pilgrimage leaders had their misgivings, the decision was made to take the king at his word. Henry invited Aske to come to court for the Christmas festivities. All was, apparently, sweetness and light.

At Snape, however, the Latimers were not able to enter wholeheartedly into the celebrations. Catherine's husband knew the king well enough not to be wholly convinced by his expressions of goodwill. He believed he would only be personally secure if he could confront Henry in person. Several of the gentlemen were hastening to the royal court to persuade the king of their loyalty. Latimer wrote to the king begging for an audience and received permission to present himself at court. He set out at the beginning of January. He had covered most of his journey and reached Buntingford, near Stevenage, when messages from the Council of the North arrived which stopped him in his tracks. He was ordered to return and be in readiness to halt any further trouble. He turned his horse around and hastened, once more, northwards. This time he got as far as Stamford, where he received even more disturbing news.

> I learn that the commons of Richmondshire, grieved at my coming [to London], have entered my house at Snape and will destroy it if I come not home shortly. If I do not please them I know not what they will do with my body and goods, my wife and children ...[10]

The rush of the gentlemen to the royal court had caused serious second thoughts on the part of some of the rebels. Despite the apparent settlement, anxiety remained and rumours abounded. When benign merchant ships arrived in Hull, word went round that they carried cannon and military supplies for use by the royal troops. Messages circulated ordering all able bodied men to be ready to assemble at an hour's notice. Catherine and her household must have been in great trepidation as hostages of such unpredictable and desperate men. Fortunately, her ordeal did not last very long. When Lord Latimer returned, he managed to persuade those who had taken possession of his home to depart. It would be pleasant – and not unreasonable – to believe that Catherine's demeanour also helped to defuse the situation.

However, the "ruffling" time, as one of Cromwell's agents described it,[11] was far from over, which was why Latimer had been sent back to Snape. The government's attitude was that the leaders of northern society should prove their loyalty by re-establishing control, rather than joining in a Gaderene *sauve-qui-peut* rush to the royal court. The embers of revolt were still smouldering and, in January, they flared up in Cumberland and in eastern Yorkshire.

The latter disturbance posed another problem for the Latimers. It occurred on their home territory in the East Riding. Worse than that, its leader was a close friend of the family. The thirty-year-old Sir Francis Bigod was one of the more remarkable figures

---

10   *L & P*, XII, pt. i, 173.
11   *L & P*, XII, pt. i, 93.

to be involved in the troubles. While in the service of Cardinal Wolsey during the late 1520s he had become an early convert to the New Learning and was extremely earnest in the Reformed faith, sponsoring preachers and personally advocating it at court and in Parliament. Bigod was close to Cromwell and an enforcement agent employed in examining the inmates of Yorkshire monasteries. He was also an enthusiastic member of the minister's propaganda team, as he stressed in a letter of 27 April 1536. He had, he informed Cromwell, set forth preachers, "at my own cost and rode all over the country with them". He had, he continued, been much mocked for his zeal but was not to be deflected from his burning ambition, which was to be an evangelist: "help me to be a priest that I may preach the word of God or else dispense with me [so] that, being no priest, I may do it". This he assured Cromwell "would please me better than all the riches of London".[12] This was the man who was so close to the Latimers that he had concluded a marriage involving his young son, Ralph, and Latimer's eleven-year-old daughter, Margaret.

How was it, then, that this Protestant zealot was, in the early days of 1537, heading a revolt which seems, at first sight, to have been part of the Pilgrimage of Grace? The answer is that he had become disillusioned – bitterly disillusioned. His support for the closure of small monasteries and the confiscation of their property rested on the understanding that the proceeds were to be used for such godly purposes as creating educational establishments. Back in the days of Wolsey's power the cardinal (enthusiastically assisted by Cromwell) had liquidated various monastic houses in order to finance the foundation of colleges in Ipswich and Oxford. This much larger dissolution must have seemed a great stride forward for the Gospel: dens of popery were to be closed down and the proceeds used to fund social and religious initiatives for the glory of God. But what had happened? King Henry was gleefully using this bonanza for his own grandiose plans and the nobility and gentry were falling over themselves to snap up desirable properties. Bigod now did a complete volte-face about the royal

---

12   *L & P*, X, 742.

supremacy. While not changing his opinion about the pope, he reached the conclusion that the king, whose role it was to bear the sword, might not be head of the English church. He stiffened the resistance of the Yorkshiremen and urged them to take and hold Scarborough and Hull until the promised parliament was called, which he, naively, believed would change the supremacy law. The Latimers might very well have thought, "With friends like this, who needs enemies?"

The new uprising played into the king's hands. The fresh outbreaks were relatively small and Norfolk and Shrewsbury had little difficulty in containing them. They also gave Henry an excuse to cancel the pardon he had previously granted and he now ordered his generals to carry out the most savage reprisals. Ringleaders were sent to London for execution so that any sympathizers in the capital could be left in no doubt that Henry Tudor could and would do exactly as he wished. As for the rank and file, 178 of them were summarily executed and their bodies exposed on gallows or suspended from church spires across the region *pour encourager les autres.*

Meanwhile, Latimer remained on tenterhooks concerning his standing with the regime. He contacted friends and relatives with access to the king and he asked Norfolk to put in a good word for him (which the duke did). One of his letters written in January when he was on the road home has survived. It was to a distant relative, Sir William Musgrave, one of the leading Cumberland gentry whose situation was, in fact, more precarious than his own. It reveals a somewhat Janus-like attitude. He asks to be recommended to Cromwell but cannot resist a dig at the minister:

> … though he be in the favour of the king, it [does not oblige] his Grace to grant what he pleases to the people, and I think his lordship would not be a hinderer of such of their desires as be reasonable.

Turning to his own participation in recent events, he goes on:

Though I durst not much contrary them, I did my best to reduce them to conformity to the king's pleasure. My being among them was a very painful and dangerous time to me; I pray God I may never see such again.[13]

Anxious months passed while Henry and Cromwell considered how to deal with all those in any way involved in the "great ruffling" and the Duke of Norfolk waited for precise instructions. It was June before Latimer's fate was decided. He was to be induced to go to London to answer in person to the king. Once again Latimer set off for the capital. He got as far as his brother's house in Essex. There he was arrested and conveyed directly to the Tower; but he was not detained long. Two factors ensured his release: one was the generous douceurs he presented to Cromwell; the other was the conspicuous loyalty of his wife's family. Norfolk reported favourably on the conduct of Catherine's brother William and her uncle (also William) who had served as the Duke of Suffolk's right-hand man throughout the rebellion. If the North was to be kept peaceable, the government would need families like the Nevilles and the Parrs.

The Askews were also falling over backwards to give proof of their loyalty. Christopher had returned to South Kelsey and, on 18 January, he and his father wrote to give Cromwell an update on the situation. They passed on information about the attacks on Hull and Scarborough. Their response, they eagerly reported, had been swift. They had sent to all the neighbouring gentry and were gathering a force ready to cross the Humber. They only waited on instructions from the king.[14] In the event, they were not called upon; the eastern Yorkshire uprising collapsed without their help.

In the aftermath of the Lincolnshire uprising the Askews were among the gentry families who were, for a time, under a cloud. Sir William had the frustration of seeing neighbours, like the Tyrrwhits and Heneages who had kept clear of trouble in 1536, profit from the considerable territorial changes that now transformed the social

---

13 *L & P*, XII, pt. i, 131.

14 *L & P*, XII, pt. i, 140.

framework of the county. As the lands of first the lesser and then the greater monasteries came on the market, other families were able to acquire vast estates. Almost all the gentlemen who profited from the Dissolution were those who had not had the misfortune to become involved with the rebels in October 1536. Two noblemen rose to prominence in Lincolnshire in the years after the uprising. One was Edward Fiennes de Clinton, Lord Clinton and Saye, who acquired large estates in the Horncastle area. The other was Charles Brandon, Duke of Suffolk. He had recently married Catherine Willoughby, the heiress of Lord Willoughby de' Eresby, and thus obtained her lands in Lincolnshire. He received grants of monastic land from the king and was also forced by Henry to exchange some of his estates in Suffolk for land in Lincolnshire. Brandon made his home at Grimsthorpe in 1537 and became the most powerful man in the county.

The Parrs' lifestyle changed considerably as a result of the Pilgrimage. Catherine's brother William was prospering at court. Thanks to his mother's skilful manoeuvring a good match had been made for him. He had been married, at the age of thirteen, to Anne Bourchier, daughter and heiress of the Earl of Essex. The union turned out to be the "marriage from hell", but it brought William considerable landed wealth and the prospect of eventually inheriting his father-in-law's title. In 1539 he was raised to the peerage as Baron Parr of Kendal. Catherine's sister, Anne, had a secure position at court as attendant on Jane Seymour and, subsequently, on Catherine Howard. In 1538 she married another courtier, William Herbert. The Latimers put the troubled North behind them, moving first to an estate in Worcestershire, then to Stowe Manor in Northamptonshire. Lord Latimer was still occasionally involved in northern politics but he now spent much time at court and in Parliament.

On 15 February 1539, one of Cromwell's agents could report to him from Lincolnshire:

> … the great ruffling is past and poor men may now live at peace with the great men. When they hear of papists' enormities to be redressed, they whisper a little, but it

is soon forgotten. People come reasonably well forward in the English paternoster since the uniform translation came down. Abbeys are now nothing pitied; the commons perceiving more common wealth to grow from their suppression, saving that they lose their prayers ... Some men of reputation keep the days abrogated work days [that is, saints days and festivals removed from the calendar], but many of the poor will not labour of those days as yet. Our valiant beggars be gone and unlawful games with them, except that in some alehouses men play at shuffleboard in default of the constables. The highways be cried out upon; every flood makes them impassable.[15]

Catherine Latimer and Anne Askew must both have hoped that now they had nothing more to worry about than poor travelling conditions.

---

15   *L & P*, XV, pt. i, 295.

CHAPTER 4

Conversion

The sixty-four-thousand-dollar question that poses itself about the lives of Catherine Parr and Anne Askew is, "What changed them?" Why did these two ladies, brought up in different environments, abandon the faith of their ancestors and embrace what would, within a few years, come to be called "Protestantism"? Though the circumstances of their environment were dissimilar they were in both instances, from a religious point of view, traditional. When the Reformation cloud, no bigger than a man's hand, first appeared in English skies, the girl who would become queen was in her teens, and the daughter of a Lincolnshire squire was still a child. Somehow, within the next few years, they had both embraced a faith which was officially heretical. Not only did they embrace it; they did so with a passion. Why? We would dearly love to know which preachers they listened to, the books they read, and the ideas they exchanged with family members and close friends. Alas, few such details have survived among the records available to us.

This is a matter of more than a little importance because it impacts, not just on the convictions of these two young ladies, but on the thoughts and beliefs of a significant number of people from the better-educated classes who lived through the tumultuous 1530s. For, however it happened, this fundamental change must have taken place during that decade. Therefore, if we can at least explore some of the influences which may have affected the deepest thoughts and feelings of Catherine and Anne we may be a step closer to discovering how the Reformation actually got under the skin of Henry VIII's England.

Let us start with education. We have already seen how, in both court and country, girls were beginning to benefit from changing attitudes towards the upbringing of both sexes, but this was only one aspect of a quiet revolution gathering momentum as Catherine and Anne grew up. In modern times, the internet has radically changed not only the way we receive and exchange information, but also our self-evaluation. We communicate through social media because we believe our ideas are important and we want to engage with others who share or reject our convictions. Five hundred years ago the printing press had the same kind of impact. The Renaissance has been called "the age of indispensable literacy".[16] What began as an exciting movement among scholars spread with astonishing rapidity through all levels of society. The more people knew, the more independent-minded they became and the more questions they asked. They realized that the concerns they had about the state of the church were widely shared.

One of the first books to come from printing presses throughout Europe was the *Manipulus Curatorum* (the "Curate's Manual"). It had been written 150 years earlier as a guide to the appropriate duties and behaviour of parish priests but the new technology had a dramatic impact on circulation. Between 1482 and 1566 it was reprinted 119 times by various presses. This manual exhorted, among other things, that parish clergy should be fully conversant with the Bible and preach it to their congregations on Sundays and festivals. The gap between this ideal and the reality could hardly have been wider. John Colet, Dean of St Paul's, in a famous address to the clergy of the southern convocation in 1512, lamented that heretics knew the Bible better than priests. Diligent bishops complained that they were obliged to appoint to livings men who could barely stumble through the Latin mass. In 1536 the Archbishop of York reported that he had no more than a dozen competent preachers in his vast diocese.

It is against this background that we must see the activities of the early reformers. Erasmus was passionate in his opposition to the clerical "closed shop" that denied lay people access to the

---

16   Barzun J. *From Dawn to Decadence*, New York, 2000, p. 54.

foundation document of the Christian faith. His Latin version of the New Testament corrected errors in the Vulgate, and, by implication, challenged the authority of the ecclesiastical establishment. He was incensed that the church's official policy was to deny lay access to the Bible while its own agents were, themselves, unwilling or incapable of expounding the Bible. It was almost as though Rome and its representatives throughout Europe had something to hide.

News of Martin Luther's challenge to the spiritual authority of the pope was widely known by 1521, the year he faced charges of heresy before the Emperor Charles V at Worms. It was a cause célèbre which provoked partisan debate at most levels of society from the royal court downwards. Henry VIII personally (with Thomas More's help) wrote a treatise attacking Luther's sacramental theology. Academics debated the issues raised by the new radicalism. But a very much wider audience was soon involved. Books and pamphlets appeared. Sermons were preached. Bold spirits gave vent to their resentment of the ecclesiastical "blind guides" who were leading the people to perdition. Equally angry responses came from men determined to defend traditional belief from the attacks of "heretics". As early as 1521 Thomas Wolsey, the king's chief minister, ordered bonfires of banned books to be lit in London and the university cities (see above pp. 15,17).

What were these books? Well, there were certainly parts of the Bible in English. William Tyndale, a young Oxford scholar, anxious that there should be an authorized, reliable vernacular version of the sacred text, tried unsuccessfully to persuade Bishop Tunstall of London to support the production of such a book. By 1524 he was on the Continent, working at his own translation, funded by radical London merchants. Two years later the first copies of his New Testament were being smuggled into England. But more specific attacks on the status quo were circulating in the radical underground. From France came François Lambert's *Farrago omnium fere rerum theologicarum*. Written in 1525 and translated into English ten years later, this draconian manifesto called for the abolition of the hierarchical organization of the Church and its replacement by a loose fraternity of local fellowships, each under its own priest or bishop. Other unorthodox thinkers had followed Tyndale into exile and sent home their own reformist tracts from the safety of cities where Protestant regimes had already been established. *Rede Me and Be Notte Wrothe* (ie. Angry) was a vigorous verse satire which attacked Wolsey and Catholic doctrines, particularly that of the mass. It was circulating in England by 1528. The same year saw the publication of Tyndale's *Parable of the Wicked Mammon*, the first round in a bruising literary conflict with Thomas More that frequently descended into ill-tempered vulgarity. Catholic satirists could be just as vigorous as their evangelical counterparts. The fashionable playwright John Heywood demonstrated this in *The Merry Play between the Pardoner and the Friar* (c.1533) which much amused the royal court when it was played before the king. At the same time an evangelical bid for influential support failed. Tristram Revel, a Cambridge graduate, sent to Anne Boleyn his translation of Lambert's *Farrago*. It was not well received but that did not deter the writer from publishing it.

But England's Reformation did not depend on the approval or otherwise of the king or his queens. It had begun long before Henry VIII began looking for a way out of his first marriage.

> It is plain that the first decade of the English Reformation produced enough matter "to set men by the ears" – enough arguments, accusations, scurrility, conviction, abuse and unsettlement to guarantee every possibility of unrest and disturbance in a country always hard to control and impossible to police efficiently.[17]

There was no escape anywhere from the reverberations of ideological conflict – whether on the edge of the Lincolnshire fens or the Yorkshire moorland.

> The theological conflicts produced by the Reformation added to and became intertwined with the existing

---

17   Elton G. R. *Policy and Police – The Enforcement of the Reformation in the Age of Thomas Cromwell*, Cambridge, 1972, p. 44.

conflicts that divided the people of early modern England. Not limited to the rarefied air of the university faculties or sniping among the religious orders, religious division and debate quickly became a feature of daily life in towns and villages across Henrician England, where the grand theological controversies of the day took on flesh in interpersonal conflicts between clergy and laity alike.[18]

By 1536, Catherine Parr and Anne Askew, as intelligent and well-educated young women, were aware of the main issues dividing traditionalists and followers of the New Learning. They were, of course, informed of the major events at the centre of national life that led eventually to the break with Rome but such information as reached them in their homes far from the capital only did so at second, third, or fourth hand via friends and relatives. Did their sympathies lie with Catherine of Aragon or Anne Boleyn? We have no way of knowing. Although Maud Parr had belonged to the entourage of Henry's first queen, Catherine rarely, if ever, met her. In later years she was close to Princess Mary but there is no evidence that their relationship predated Catherine's taking on the role of step-mother to Henry's children.

The only direct involvement of Catherine and Anne with the dramatic events of the 1530s was their frightening confrontation with the rebels in 1536–37. It was worrying enough to have unruly mobs going through their houses questioning their servants about the loyalties of their employers and searching for evidence that might be incriminating, but there were other issues of deeper concern. How far could they rely on their own servants and tenants? To what extent had their standing with the king been compromised? As we have seen, life did settle down after 1537, though the Latimers distanced themselves from the troubled North. But the memories lingered. Catherine and Anne may well have equated religious traditionalism with leering peasants, egged on by belligerent clergy, all intent on retaining the monasteries and

---

18   Gunther K. *Reformation Unbound – Protestant Vision of Reform in England, 1525–1590*, Cambridge, 2014, p. 64.

ancient rituals, even if that meant the breakdown of civil order. This, after all, seemed to support Henrician propaganda. In 1534 the king's printer, Thomas Swinnerton, had asked in the pamphlet *A Litel Treatise ageynst the mutterynge of some papists in corners*, "Who be the occasion and stirrers up of war and strife, in Christendom but the pope and papists?" It was, he insisted, they who set nation against nation and clergy against laity.[19]

As they contemplated their own convictions and their own self-interest, the ladies can scarcely have avoided pondering deeper questions. What did they believe about the royal supremacy and the loyalty of subjects; and papal authority; and the importance of monasticism; and the role of the clergy as guardians of religious truth? And what, fundamentally, was religious truth? We know the opinions they eventually came to hold on these matters, opinions that imperilled their very lives, but we do not know how they came by those opinions. In the absence of documentary evidence the next best source of information is the lives and beliefs of people we *do* know about and who were in a position to influence both our leading ladies.

Let us make a start with that strange figure, Sir Francis Bigod, who, as we know, was close to the Latimers. Not only had the two parties pledged themselves to a marriage union, Latimer also came to Bigod's aid with a loan when the young man was in serious financial difficulties. Bigod seems to have been won over to Lutheranism while studying at Oxford in the early 1520s by the proselytizing activities of Thomas Garrett, a colporteur of banned books who targeted students. His technique was to offer extra-curricular tuition to undergraduates desiring help with Greek and Hebrew and then to open up the Bible and point out its lack of support for official dogma. Garrett fell foul of the authorities, was forced to recant his "heresies", and spent some uncomfortable months in an Oxford gaol. After this he went to ground for a while but when the king's "great matter" opened up the opportunity for anti-papal preaching, Garrett resumed his activities. Now he had the support of Francis Bigod who employed him as a personal chaplain and set him to

---

19   Gunther 2014, p. 66.

preach the Gospel. Bigod believed passionately in preaching. Around 1535, he ventured into print with a modest volume entitled *A Treatise concerning Impropriations of Benefices*. He denounced abbots and senior clergy who accumulated livings which should have supported full-time parish priests who would properly exercise the cure of souls and, specifically, preach regularly from their pulpits. The author knew well what he was complaining about because, in his native Yorkshire, which had 622 parishes, 392 were impropriated and served by ill-paid and often ignorant curates, performing the bare minimum of their pastoral responsibilities. Bigod was passionate for the *reformation* of the system and this explains his genuine distress when he discovered that what Henry and Cromwell had in mind was not the correction of a corrupt institution but its overthrow – and not to use the proceeds for advancing the Gospel but for filling the royal coffers.[20] Bigod had not changed his basic evangelical stance. Although he ended up prolonging what began as a conservative rebellion, there was an intellectual consistency about his position. Unfortunately, he was politically naive, and he paid for that with his life. His last letter to Cromwell demonstrates his continuing commitment to the New Learning, a commitment he still believed that Cromwell shared. In it he commends two associates who were friends of the Gospel:

> I beseech your good lordship whether I live or die to be good lord to Master [William] Jerome, who in few words, both for preaching and [blank] hath for fellows ... In like case, for God's sake, help [?] Cervington, who in my country dare not come because he is a true favourer of God's word.[21]

---

20 Bigod was not alone as a genuine reformer discovering too late the direction being taken by royal policy. Anne Boleyn had been among those who presumed to question her husband's intentions – with fatal consequences.

21 Dickens A. G. *Lollards and Protestant in the Diocese of York 1509–1558*, Hull, 1959, pp. 103–4.

In 1540 Jerome was burned as a heretic along with Thomas Garrett. All we know of Cervington is that he was later an associate of the Protestant apologist, John Bale.

Bigod's career warns us against oversimplifying the religious conflict of the mid-Tudor years. We cannot label individuals simply as "Catholic" or "Protestant". People took varied stances on the political and religious issues of the day and had to weigh up several factors – obedience to the Crown, reaction of neighbours, attitude towards the clergy, understanding of the Bible, and so forth. What we can say with confidence is that many prominent people, certainly including Lady Latimer, were exposed to the new teaching by hearing radical preachers, talking with friends and relatives and by clandestinely reading Tyndale's New Testament. Catherine was exposed to the New Learning as much as most ladies of her class and more than many of them. She can hardly have failed to encounter the beliefs of Bigod and his entourage of preachers. And at some point in the midst of all her troubles she turned from formal, ritualized, traditional worship to a close study of the New Testament, as she later explained:

> I never knew Christ for my Saviour and Redeemer until
> this time … many have this opinion, saying "Who knoweth
> not there is a Christ? Who … doth not confess Him
> his Saviour?" … believing their dead, human, historical
> faith and knowledge (which they have learned in their
> scholastical books) to be the true, infused faith … true it is,
> except they have this [infused] faith … they shall never be
> justified … I have certainly no curious learning to defend
> this matter withal, but a simple zeal and earnest love to the
> truth, inspired by God, who promiseth to pour His Spirit
> upon all flesh which I have, by the grace of God, whom I
> most humbly honour, felt in myself to be true.[22]

---

22   *The Lamentation of a Sinner*, in J. Mueller (ed.) *Katherine Parr – Complete Works and Correspondence*, Chicago, 2011, pp. 458–59.

Though Catherine nowhere in her writings revealed the precise circumstances of her conversion, it is difficult to believe that it was not a dramatic, comparatively sudden occurrence, a moment of enlightenment, such as that which had befallen the monk, Martin Luther, as a result of studying the opening of St Paul's argument in his Letter to the Romans:

> I began to understand the justice [righteousness] of God as that by which the just lives by the gift of God, namely by faith, and this sentence, "The justice [righteousness] of God is revealed in the Gospel," to be that passive justice, with which the merciful God justifies us by faith, as it is written, "The just lives by faith". This straightway made me feel as though reborn, and as though I had entered by open gates into paradise itself.[23]

Catherine's very words have a Lutheran feel about them. Her description of her motive for writing, "a simple zeal and earnest love to the truth" echo the opening words of Luther's "95 Theses", "Out of a love and zeal for the truth and the desire to bring it to light ..." Whether she had read the document which had set all Christendom by the ears or heard Luther's words declaimed by a preacher such as William Jerome is unknown but the whole tenor of her proclamation of justification by faith clearly had its origin in the Wittenberg monk.

Other phrases also provide evidence of the German reformer's teaching, much of which was circulating, at second hand, by English evangelicals. Terms such as "historical faith" are reminiscent of Tyndale's written debate with Thomas More. In his *Answer to More* of 1532, he had contrasted the belief that was mere intellectual assent with "feeling faith ... written in thine heart ... because the Spirit of God so preacheth and so testifieth unto thy soul ... that thou shalt be saved through Christ".[24] There can be little doubt

---

23 Rupp G. *The Righteousness of God*, New York, 1953, p. 122.

24 Walter H. (ed.) *An Answer to Sir Thomas More's Dialogue*, Cambridge, 1850, pp. 55–56.

that Catherine had followed the running debate between the humanist who had influenced her early education and the exiled scholar whose books formed part of the intellectual food of her recent years. Few women of Catherine's station were better informed of issues dividing scholars in the 1530s and it takes very little imagination to see her own thinking reaching its moment of crisis amidst the traumatic events of 1536–37.

In trying to assess the religious influences brought to bear on Anne Askew we have less to go on. Hers was a domestic existence and she soon had something else to think about. By the time the rebellion was over she was very much of marriageable age and it was soon after the "ruffling" that she left her father's house for that of a new husband, Thomas Kyme, of Friskney – deep in the fenland to the far south-west. Friskney and South Kelsey were in the same county but they might as well have been on different continents. Instead of the wooded slopes of the wolds and the meadows along the Ancholme, Anne's window now looked out over a vast, unrelieved landscape of marsh and dyke. Instead of friendly, familiar people, always ready to show her the respect due to her station, she was surrounded by unknown and unknowable, taciturn peasants, who regarded her as a stranger and would continue to regard her so if she lived in their midst to the age of ninety. Instead of educated conversation with well-bred relatives and friends, acquainted in some measure with a fashionable world, she had for companions neighbours whose book-learning was non-existent, whose knowledge (and interest) did not extend beyond the care of their fields and flocks. This was the area in which the Lincolnshire uprising had been born. One of Kyme's relatives was among the ringleaders executed for his part in it. For Anne, still in her teens, the abrupt change of lifestyle must have come as a shock. It was not helped by the circumstances surrounding her marriage. It was, of course, an arranged affair agreed between the fathers of the young couple but Anne's involvement had come about because of a family tragedy. Originally, it was her elder sister, Martha, who had been pledged to Thomas Kyme, but the chosen bride had died before the wedding could be held. In order not to waste all the arrangements that had been made, it was agreed that Anne should step into her dead sister's shoes. We will return to her plight later. But first we will probe her background in the immediate aftermath of rebellion.

Sir William Askew's main concern was to prove his loyalty to the regime and to dispel any doubts created by his handling of the recent crisis. Religious conviction and self-preservation combined to make him throw himself fervently into the work of furthering Cromwell's policies. In doing so he alienated some of his shire colleagues who considered him to be overzealous in his persecution of Catholics and accused him, on the other hand, of harbouring and supporting heretics. Though this charge was undoubtedly exaggerated, it seems that evangelical preachers and anti-clerical elements knew Sir William as a lenient justice.

In the summer of 1538 matters came to a head between Sir William Askew and his colleagues on the commission for the peace in Lindsey. The constable of Barrow upon Humber, one James Clarke, as the man responsible for the preservation of law and order in the town from day to day, was particularly sensitive to potential troublemakers who showed scant respect for authority – including ecclesiastical authority. When, therefore, he received a complaint from no less a person than the abbot of Thornton Abbey that a certain Thomas Bawmborough of Barrow had used "proud words" against him, he took action. Bawmborough was apprehended and brought before the justices at the next sessions. He was quite unrepentant and had only himself to blame that he was not dismissed, for when Thomas Dymock, from the bench, said to him, "Get thee hence, there is over many such busy fellows in the county as thou art," Bawmborough retorted "with a proud stomach", "By God's blood, there will be more before there be fewer." Bawmborough was marked out for reference to a higher court.

There the matter might have ended had not the offender's father, Laurence Bawmborough, taken up the cudgels on his son's behalf. He bitterly resented the action of his officious constable and the judgment of the commission of the peace. "This doing is appalling," he complained to Clarke, "and I trust this world will amend it." The constable quickly tired of the aggrieved father's complaints, as also of the whispering and finger-pointing of citizens who took the Bawmboroughs' part. When he could stand it no longer he took Laurence Bawmborough before the nearest justice, without waiting for the next sessions. That justice happened to be Sir William who was staying at the time at Stallingborough. Under existing law it was a criminal offence to criticize the workings of the king's courts and Clarke now applied to have Bawmborough arrested for uttering heinous words. He had not allowed for Sir William's complete lack of patience with pompous abbots, heresy hunters, self-important minor officials or commotions over petty matters. The elderly knight listened with increasing ill-temper as the two men stood before him accusing, excusing, alleging, and denying. At length he cut them short with an oath and sent them packing: "Get you home and agree together, for you will never let till one of you undo another."

Laurence Bawmborough was jubilant but Clarke was a tenacious enemy and moreover he knew who to go to next – a man who would listen to him sympathetically for no other reason than that Sir William Askew had turned him down. The constable was quite within his rights to appeal from one justice of the peace to another. He, therefore, presented his case and his man to Sir Robert Tyrrwhit, who found that Laurence Bawmborough *had* spoken heinous words and, in defiance of Askew, committed the man to Lincoln Castle. Clarke was triumphant and resolved to strike while the iron was hot and, at the next meeting of the quarter sessions at Caistor in August, he brought forward more suspected heretics, including Robert Hanschey (alias Smith) and one Teynby. One look at the document was sufficient to convince Askew that the constable of Barrow was making unnecessary trouble. He resolved on a rather naive method to try to stop the accused coming to trial: he put the charge sheet in his purse, doubtless hoping that this case would be overlooked in the press of other business. When Clarke appeared to pursue his charge, Sir William claimed that he had heard nothing about these two men and that certainly the constable had not formally presented written accusation against them. This subterfuge failed when the other justices, Sir Robert Tyrrwhit, Sir Thomas Dymock, Sir

John Heneage, William Dalyson, and Robert Dighton, insisted on hearing the case. When the details were presented, Sir William did his best to persuade his colleagues of the utter futility of the case but again found himself up against Tyrrwhit who swayed the other justices with the result that Hanschey, Teynby, and others were sentenced to the pillory. The indignant Sir William restrained himself until the hearings were over and the members of the commission had retired to private chambers, then he told his fellows just what he thought of the day's proceedings. The punishment meted out to the offenders was excessive and wholly without precedent. On the contrary, retorted Tyrrwhit, express orders had come from the king for the punishment of such offenders. At this point Sir William lost his temper, vehemently accusing his enemies on the commission of partiality: "You were only severe with these men because I tried to help them." To which Heneage retorted, "That was foolishly spoken." If Askew's blood was up now, so was Tyrrwhit's. "It is you who are to blame for maintaining such lewd fellows. Barrow has never been quiet ever since you have borne any rule there." At this point the two men would have come to blows had the others not intervened. As it was, the meeting broke up with Askew and Tyrrwhit mouthing threats and counter-threats. In the event it was Sir Robert who took further action, sending a full – though one-sided – report to Cromwell. The Council does not appear to have taken action immediately, but these events can hardly have failed (as, indeed, they were intended) to discredit Sir William Askew further in the eyes of the government.[25] Such incidents leave us in no doubt as to where Askew's sympathies lay as religious discord continued to smoulder among the embers of a divided society.

We cannot draw firm lines on a map to demarcate "traditionalist" and "progressive", "Catholic" and "evangelical" areas, but it is certainly clear that several factors could combine to give some tracts of country their own distinct religious flavour. Thus, it was characteristic of the fenland, because of the inherent difficulties of travel, that communities tended to be introverted and unreceptive

---

25   *L&P*, XIII, pt ii, 245(1).

of new ideas. Here the church was a dominant social force. Lincolnshire could boast fifty-one major religious houses and over thirty friaries and smaller religious foundations.

By contrast, Nottinghamshire was home to ten monasteries, one nunnery and four friaries. It was also bisected by the Trent which was navigable to seagoing craft as far as Nottingham and beyond. The great multinational Hanseatic League had an outpost at Hull, from where its representatives made their way upriver, sometimes carrying Tyndale's New Testament and other banned books among their merchandise. Only ten years had passed since Thomas More carried out a raid on the Steelyard, the Hanse's London headquarters, in his search for illicit literature. At smaller ports there was less vigilance and the trend of religious policy under Cromwell encouraged colporteurs to be bolder. But, in any case, the area between the Trent and the Don had an old and ongoing reputation for religious radicalism. There had been Lollard cells here within living memory and, eighty years later, much of the impetus for the settlement of Puritan colonies in the New World came from this locality.

If we need evidence of the prevailing mood in the area, a cause célèbre which ran throughout the summer and early autumn of 1537 provides it. There was in Rotherham a group of heretics, of a largely traditional, Lollard persuasion. Most of them were sufficiently circumspect to keep out of trouble – until 1537. Then, perhaps emboldened by the new trends in official religious policy, one of them, William Senes, a choirmaster in the song school at Jesus College, spoke out. On 4 May he was in the parish church when he saw a priest, Thomas Pylley, in the chantry of Henry Carnbull, saying a mass for the soul of the donor and sprinkling holy water on his tomb. Senes ridiculed these acts as superstitious and soon found himself engaged in debate with the clergy of the college. He urged the new doctrines as enshrined in the English New Testament and said that men were now freed from old papist errors. The argument rapidly grew more heated. William Ingram, the parish clerk of Rotherham, angrily retorted that he believed what his father had believed. This was too much for the ardent disciple of Tyndale. "Thy father was a liar and is in hell," he retorted. "And so is my father in hell also; my father never knew Scripture and now it is come forth." From this point the contest degenerated into a slanging match.

This event sparked off a controversy between the priests and the members of Senes's group, more of whom became involved in incidents during the following weeks. On several occasions Senes was confronted with irate conservative opinion, but the contests were not always between orthodoxy and heresy. In one conversation the choirmaster accused his adversaries of disloyalty to the king.

Thomas Holden, a chantry priest, and Mr Drapper, a chaplain at Jesus College, apparently upheld the Lincolnshire rebels: "… those was good lads, for they would put down those heretics Cromwell, Cranmer and Latimer …" Senes remarked that these were traitorous words and cited such notable figures as the Earl of Shrewsbury and Sir John Markham, the most substantial landowner in the area, as among those who agreed with the king's policy and were carrying it out. The two priests were, by this time, thoroughly angry; they dismissed the Earl as "nought" and Markham as a "heretic". These arguments ended in the usual way with such expressions as "Sir John Lack-learning" and "Whoreson knave" flying back and forth.

After several incidents the bailiff of Rotherham had to intervene in the interests of keeping the peace. He arrested Senes and two colleagues and set them before the Earl of Shrewsbury at Sheffield Castle. Senes was charged with holding heretical opinions and possessing banned books. The reception he received from the aged Earl was hardly encouraging.

"Come near, thou heretic and kneel near. Ha! Thou heretic, thou hast books?"

"Yes, my Lord. The New Testament I have," replied the cowed Senes.

"The New Testament thou hast is nought," retorted the angry and almost incoherent nobleman. "Thou art an heretic, and but for shame I should thrust my dagger into thee!"

With little more ado the Earl had the unfortunate trio clapped in prison and handed their case over to the archbishop's court.

During the following weeks Senes's friends and relations did all they could to help him. One of them, John Babington, from a gentry family based at Kingston-on-Soar, had loose contact with Cromwell. A message to London had the case moved to the court of King's Bench, where it was quashed.[26]

Such incidents show that the defeat of popular Catholic reaction in 1536–37 had not silenced grassroots opposition. Back in London, Cromwell was very aware that resistance could flare up anywhere and at any time. For now he had the initiative and he had to press it home, firmly and without delay. The year 1538 saw the climax of the Cromwellian Reformation. In foreign affairs the Master Secretary tried to steer the king into an alliance with the German Lutheran princes of the Schmalkalde League. At home he exterminated a group of noblemen whose Yorkist connections and conservative opinions constituted, in his view, a threat to the throne. And he completed the demolition of monasticism. Now that no one would dare to come to their aid, the assault on the larger religious houses moved ahead rapidly.

Cromwell received the voluntary submission of many religious houses whose superiors accurately read the writing on the wall and yielded up their lands and goods in the hope of gaining royal favour and fat pensions rather than wait until they were forcibly dispossessed. At the same time, pockets of papalist resistance were ruthlessly sought out. There was a full-scale onslaught made on images, shrines, and other "objects of superstition". Throughout the country rood lofts and statues, ruthlessly exposed "miracle-working" relics, and shrines and were mercilessly torn down. On the positive side, the vicar general issued fresh injunctions in September stressing the educative role of the clergy and announcing his grand scheme for the setting up of an English Bible in every parish church.

This activity relied heavily on an army of agents in the shires, men of substance and authority in the localities who enthusiastically supported the reform out of conviction or self-interest or a mixture of the two. In the Trent Valley the dominant clique was led by Sir John Markham of Cottam, whom we have already met. He had

---

26   Dickens 1959, pp. 37ff.

done service for several years in the royal court, was a Member of Parliament for the county and was, on several occasions, Sheriff of Nottingham. Among Markham's friends and supporters were the Babingtons of Kingston-upon-Soar, the Hercys of Grove, and the Lascelles of Gateford and Sturton-le-Steeple.

There can be little doubt about the religious allegiance of the Babingtons. One litmus test is the wording of wills. In these "final" documents in which testators often gave unequivocal expression to their beliefs, several chose to abandon the traditional opening which ran something like this, "I bequeath my soul into the hands of Almighty God, beseeching the blessed Virgin Mary and all the saints to pray for me", in preference for more personal declarations of faith which had no need for intermediaries. Sir Anthony Babington's will of 1536 was a classic example of this trend: "I commit and bequeath my soul to God, my Master and Redeemer, trusting in his grace and by the merits of Christ's passion and resurrection, in whose faith I do believe and by his grace will die to be one of the number of such as shall be saved."[27] John Babington, Anthony's younger son, had no scruples about investigating and punishing those who opposed the new order. In the spring of 1538 he joined Sir John Markham in examining Ralph Swenson of Lenton Priory for seditious words spoken about the king. Swenson was duly hanged.

The Hercy and Lascelles families were especially close. The three Lascelles children, George, John, and Mary, had been orphaned in 1520 and were brought up by their relatives and neighbours, Humphrey and Elizabeth Hercy. George eventually took over the running of the family estate, John followed the conventional educational route for sons of the gentry – a couple of years at Oxford, followed by time at the inns of court. The objectives of this training were the learning of enough law to equip him as a future justice of the peace and a member of royal commissions and also the acquiring of useful connections. What membership

---

27   Principal Probate Registry. F.39 Hogen, c.f. J. W. Clay (ed.) *North Country Wills*, I, Publications of the Surtees Society, Volume cxvi, pp. 100–101.

of the law schools in Holborn did not officially provide was tutoring in heresy but that was precisely what they were becoming notorious for. There was ancient rivalry between students of civil law and canon law and frequent arguments over the respective jurisdiction of royal and ecclesiastical courts. This tended to make the young barristers and solicitors in training receptive to radical literature which challenged the church. The circulation among them of banned books was a constant source of annoyance to the Bishop of London and his officers. Whether John Lascelles was won over to evangelicalism at Furnival's Inn or whether he arrived in London already committed to Bible-based faith we do not know, but it is clear that, by the time he was out of his teens, he was committed to the New Learning. It was probably through family influence that John was drawn to Cromwell's attention. He was soon being employed by the minister in carrying messages to and from his associates in the Midlands, messages that left little doubt about the sympathies of the group. For instance, in May 1538 Sir John Hercy (now head of the family) sent this via John Lascelles:

> I have been informed that Sir Edward Eland, Chaplain to Dr Knolys, Vicar of Wakefield, has been teaching young folks seditious songs against your Lordship and others. This he has confessed. Let me know your pleasure in this by your servant John Lascelles, to whom I beg you to continue good Lord … Have pity for the poor men of Cottam, sore vexed by Anthony Neville, who, besides his own matter, threatens them with a lunatic priest put to them by the Archbishop of York's officers. They showed themselves loyal at the commotion time. I wish you would be pleased to take the Lady at Doncaster away, and send some good preachers into the country.[28]

The next step in John Lascelles' career was preferment to royal service. He became an attendant in the Privy Chamber, in regular contact with the king and the leading men and women in the land.

---

28   *L & P*, XIII, pt. i, 387–8.

His sister, too, was going up in the world. By 1538 she had a place in the entourage of Agnes Howard, Dowager Duchess of Norfolk. Her duties included tending the needs of several young ladies of noble birth who were entrusted to her care for finishing their education. Among them was the fifteen-year-old Catherine Howard.

Sir William Askew did not have such an easy ride as his friends on the other side of the county boundary. A year after the Caistor incident he was again in trouble, not this time for being lenient but (in the eyes of his opponents) overzealous. The priest of the chantry of St Helen's at Croft, a fenland village near Wainfleet, was reported to him for offences under the Act of Supremacy. Sir William sent for the man, examined him and committed him to prison. As soon as his enemies heard of this they wrote protesting at his overzealousness to Cromwell. The vicar general had received a string of complaints about Sir William, stretching over several months, and had already written to South Kelsey urging the knight to appear before the Council to answer charges against him. Cromwell was no friend of papists but he had no intention of putting the weight of the government behind a Midland justice who was, apparently, causing considerable trouble in the locality. He ordered Sir William to set the chantry priest free. Furious, Askew obeyed, pointing out to Cromwell that he did so "notwithstanding good reason for expulsion, as thou shalt know hereafter".[29]

Sir Robert Tyrrwhit continued his personal vendetta, making frequent complaints to Cromwell of Askew's overzealous hounding of suspected papists. Eventually, in December 1539, the minister yielded to their pleas and summoned Sir William to answer for his behaviour to the Council. Askew pleaded ill-health and this seems not to have been mere prevarication, for he took to his bed soon after and died a year later, following a long and painful illness. By this time, Thomas Cromwell himself was dead.

So, we return to Anne Askew or, as she now was, Anne Kyme, isolated from family and friends in distant Friskney. The legends that revolve around her in these early years of her marriage are not supported by any documentary evidence but, as later events

29   *L & P*, XV, 601.

demonstrated, her union with Thomas Kyme was not a happy one, and one reason for this was Anne's "gospelling" activity. The word was a new and hastily invented one to explain a novel phenomenon. In 1539 Cromwell had pulled off his biggest coup, the issuing of the Great Bible. Henry had, at last, sanctioned this translation and ordered it to be set up in every parish church. Evangelicals had long been hoping and praying for this day and, now that all sanctions had been removed, several took it upon themselves to be proclaimers of Holy Scripture. They gathered groups around them in the churches to hear God's word in their mother tongue. They did not lack for audiences. Illiterate and semi-literate parishioners who had been bemused by all the controversy surrounding banned Bibles were naturally eager to hear for themselves what all the fuss was about. As mistress of the house, Anne probably regarded it as her right and duty to explain the Gospel to her servants. This did not please Kyme or the local clergy, but they were in a difficult position. The royal order authorizing the translation had required incumbents to place the book "in some convenient place within the church that he have care of, whereas your parishioners may most commodiously resort to the same and read it".

So we can now attempt an answer to the question with which we began this chapter: when and how did Anne become a believer in the reformed faith? It is clear from her later history that she was a high-spirited young woman. It is also obvious that she went through some harrowing experiences during and after the Lincolnshire uprising. We may add to this the reasonable conjecture that she was well informed of the theological arguments that were dividing the nation and that she may have owned a copy of Tyndale's New Testament. It seems clear that she had come to her new religious allegiance before her marriage, otherwise she would not have defied her husband. As it was, persecution only strengthened her resolve, for was it not a sombre truth that those who followed the crucified Christ were destined to share his sufferings?

CHAPTER 5

Three Weddings and a Funeral

Thomas Cromwell's prodigious industry is truly remarkable. He planned legislation and steered it through Parliament; he was careful to maintain his influence at court; he received a stream of ambassadors and other important visitors; and, as we have seen, he was daily in contact with his agents in every corner of the realm. Cromwell was a driven man; nothing else will adequately explain his punishing work schedule. He was bent on nothing less than changing England and England's people – how they were governed, how they worshipped, what they believed. He was very clear in his mind about what he wanted to achieve and how he was going to achieve it. As 1539 drew to its close he could reflect that his Promethean task was close to completion. The Great Bible had been delivered to churches throughout the realm and chained to reading desks so that dyed-in-the-wool traditionalists could not easily spirit it away. The king's subjects now had access to it themselves and any layman could check what his priests were telling him. And now a Lutheran princess was on her way to be married to England's King Henry, a widower since the death of Jane Seymour in 1537.

This was important for various diplomatic reasons. It would free Henry from imperial apron strings and strengthen the Protestant German princes in their dealings with Charles V. But it had domestic implications also. Henry was determined to remarry. If his choice was to fall, once again, on a homegrown consort this would change the balance of power within the court. The new queen's relatives would expect and receive lands, titles, offices, and other marks of royal favour. They would become the new cocks of the walk and if their policies did not agree with those of the Master Secretary his position would be seriously undermined. It was important, therefore, that Henry's fourth wife should come from outside the realm. But the king was fussy. He insisted on staging a beauty contest. Ambassadors were quizzed on the physical attributes of potential brides, and the royal painter, Hans Holbein, was sent to capture likenesses of the most suitable candidates. The French king echoed the thoughts of many when he likened his brother monarch's proceedings at having royal ladies paraded before him to those of a coper vetting mares at a horse fair. But Cromwell proved himself an accomplished dealer; by careful editing of ambassadorial reports and "advising" Holbein of how best to present his portraits he had persuaded the king to conclude negotiations with the Duke of Cleves, Julich, for the marriage of his sister.

Catherine Parr's family had cause to welcome the latest developments. They had survived the royal marriage turbulence of the last decade. 1539 was a particularly good year for her siblings, who became well-established at court. Anne, thanks to her marriage to the King's favourite, William Herbert, and her appointment as chief gentlewoman to the queen was a fixture in the royal household. William, Baron Parr of Kendal, was well liked by Henry and often found in the royal quarters.

The next few years were the quietest of Catherine's life. She probably enjoyed the rural calm of Stowe Manor, a few miles west of Northampton and, if she craved more excitement she could visit her brother and sister at the royal court. However, the way things were going she might well have wanted to keep her distance. In the years 1540 to 1543 political life took a very nasty turn – or, rather, a series of very nasty turns. Henry VIII recognized, probably for the first time, the genies that he had let out of the bottle. It would not be until Christmas Eve 1545 that he made a tearful speech to Parliament on the subject of religious discord but the truth of the situation must have been coming gradually clearer over the preceding years. Henry complained:

> … what charity is amongst you, when the one calleth the
> other heretic and Anabaptist, and he calleth him in turn
> papist, hypocrite and Pharisee … you of the clergy preach

one against another, teach contrary to one another, criticize one another without charity or discretion … Alas, how can the poor souls live in concord when you preachers sow amongst them, in your sermons, debate and discord? From you they look for light, and you bring them to darkness … you of the temporality are not clean and unspotted of malice and envy; for you rail on bishops, speak slanderously of priests, and rebuke and taunt preachers, both contrary to good order and Christian fraternity … although you are permitted to read holy scripture and to have the word of God in your mother tongue, you must understand that it is licensed you so to do only to inform your own conscience and to instruct your children and family and not to make scripture a railing and taunting stock … I am very sorry to know and hear how unreverently that most precious jewel, the word of God, is disputed, rhymed, sung and jangled in every alehouse and tavern contrary to the true meaning and doctrine of the same; and yet I am even as much sorry that the readers of the same follow it, in doing, so faintly and coldly. For of this I am sure, that charity was never so faint amongst you, and virtuous and godly living was never less used, nor was God himself amongst Christians, never less reverenced, honoured or served …[30]

Henry, of course, did not blame himself for the fragmenting of his country into warring camps. To him it was clear that he had fulfilled his religious obligations. He prided himself on having given a spiritual lead to his people. He had checked the papalist backlash of 1536–37. He had provided his subjects with their own vernacular Bible. As bishops and scholars hammered out the official doctrine of the English church in the 1530s and 1540s, the king was closely involved in their deliberations. The results were published in successive treatises and Acts of Parliament: *Articles Devised by the King's Highness's Majesty to Establish Christian Quietness*

---

30   Stow J. *Annals of the Reformation*, 1601, p. 590.

and Unity Among Us (1536); *The Bishops' Book* (1537*);* the Act of Six Articles (1539); the Act for the Advancement of True Religion (1543). These declarations of "Christian truth" were the results of contentious controversy between Catholic traditionalists, Catholic humanist reformists and evangelicals, all under Henry's eagle eye. In legal terms they clarified what Henry's subjects were supposed to believe. In reality they established nothing. What was set down on paper could be, and was, overridden by necessities of state policy, the spread of grassroots heresy and the changing moods of the king.

At the beginning of 1540 Cromwell had seemed to be secure in the driving seat but the king's well-known reaction to Anne of Cleves was a powerful solvent of the trust Henry placed in his minister. His bride did not stimulate him sexually (although he did not call her a "Flanders mare") and she lacked the sophistication and courtly accomplishments Henry had come to expect in his queens. Cromwell's enemies took advantage of this chink in his armour. The Bishop of Winchester, Stephen Gardiner, and the Duke of Norfolk dangled before the disillusioned, sex-starved king Norfolk's niece, Catherine Howard. The vivacious seventeen-year-old was everything Anne was not and Henry had to have her. Shifts in the diplomatic cloudscape also removed the desirability of an alliance with the Lutheran princes. In the summer of 1540 everything went into reverse – or so it seemed. Henry escaped from his fourth marriage and embarked on his fifth. The hated Thomas Cromwell went to the block. The king was like a new man with his still-teenage bride and the party of reaction set about their plans to build on their newly strengthened foundation.

But Henry demonstrated that he was not to be taken for granted. On 30 July 1540, just two days after his marriage, he delivered a gruesome lesson on the importance of religious unity. Three of Cromwell's closest associates in the work of reform, Thomas Gerrard, William Jerome, and Robert Barnes, were burned as heretics at Smithfield. A few metres away three obdurate Catholics were hanged, drawn, and quartered as traitors for having denied the royal supremacy. The point could not have been more clearly and dramatically made, for Smithfield had never before been chosen for the despatching of traitors. Days later, four men who had previously been imprisoned by Cromwell on suspicion of participating in a Catholic plot were also judged guilty of treason and similarly despatched.

Meanwhile, traditionalist activists, buoyed by Cromwell's fall, set about their nationwide purge of men who had been closely associated with the late minister. If contemporary calculations are to be believed, hundreds of victims found themselves imprisoned on suspicion of heresy. This was a major initiative by Gardiner, Norfolk, and their aides to reverse everything Cromwell, Cranmer, and their friends had achieved. Their tool was the Act of Six Articles, which had endorsed major Catholic doctrines, specifically transubstantiation. Here, for the first time, we have clear evidence of the conservatives' frantic determination to halt the progress of the Reformation in England at all costs. It is important to understand their passion and determination for, throughout the last years of the reign, it was these that drove them to attempt the destruction of the archbishop, reformists at court, and, eventually Queen Catherine Parr.

But they were baulked by the king. Quite what was going on in Henry's mind during the high summer of 1540 is difficult to fathom. In the following spring the French ambassador Charles de Marillac described him as driven by his pain to great rages during which he railed against his councillors who were only interested in their own profit and, indeed, against his grumbling people whom he was determined to make so poor that they would have neither the boldness nor the power to oppose him. Yet such outbursts did not represent any consistent policy and, Marillac learned from his informants, Henry's opinions were quite capable of making a 180-degree turn between morning and evening. Those close to the king certainly took advantage of his mood swings and he was quick to blame his mistakes on poor advice from his council. It was Marillac who, in his reports to Paris, famously blamed the liars of his court circles for persuading him to get rid of Cromwell, "the most faithful servant he ever had".[31] The ambassador was far

---

31 *L & P*, XVI, 589–90.

from being an unbiased witness, but his description of Henry's changeability ties in well with evidence from other observers. Henry VIII was a creature of contrasts. He was a shrewd judge of character, capable of sound, considered judgment. Yet he was also given to rash outbursts and impulsive decisions.

One fact fully appreciated by all those who understood the king was the importance of personal contact. Anyone who was in Henry's bad books knew that the only way to regain royal favour was to seek an audience. The king, it seems, was a sucker for the grovelling apology and enjoyed displaying his gracious clemency. According to a London merchant, Richard Hilles, who fled to Strasbourg in the immediate aftermath of Cromwell's fall, this was how the brake was firmly applied to the Six Articles persecution:

> ... very many persons, especially the preachers of the
> gospel, were imprisoned in every part of England; and at
> London four or five of the principal of them. They made
> search too after Doctor Crome, a man of great gravity and
> wisdom, (who, together with Latimer, was the first who
> in our times sowed the pure doctrine of the gospel;) he,
> when he heard ... that he was denounced, went privately to
> the palace, and falling on his knees before the king, (after
> he had first informed him of the cruel treatment of some
> preachers and citizens at London,) prayed him for God's
> sake to put a stop to these severities, and of his wisdom and
> godliness to apply a remedy. The king forthwith gave order,
> that no further persecution should take place on account
> of religion, and that those who were then in prison should
> be set at liberty, upon their friends giving security for their
> appearance whenever they should be called for. The king,
> probably, was partly induced to grant this indulgence, in
> the hope that when these things were once set at rest, and
> the old errors (as he considered them) forgiven, the people
> would be more quiet and obedient in future.[32]

---

32   Robinson H. (ed.) *Original Letters Relative to the English Reformation*, Cambridge, 1846, p. 208.

Edward Crome was one of the leading London preachers and vicar of St Mary Aldermary. He was one of the evangelicals who sailed very close to the wind. Though boldly asserting his beliefs and being arrested on at least two occasions, he was adroit enough, when push came to shove, to avoid dire punishment. He was not of the stuff from which martyrs are made. Others were not so fortunate. There were some categories of believers who were exempt from the general pardon of 1540.

And that brings us to what was happening at grassroots level: confusion. England's religious life was a microcosm of the religious life of mainland Europe. The competing ecclesiologies underlying the northern crisis of 1536–37 did not tell the whole story. The nation was not simply divided between Catholics and Protestants, or traditionalists and "New Learners", or supporters of the king and disciples of the pope, or reformed and unreformed believers. Different strands of theological thinking competed for the allegiance of those men and women who thought at all about these things. We must also take note of the fact that people's convictions developed and changed – sometimes rapidly – in these years. Catherine Parr's circle, with its strong court connections, was largely comprised of people who supported the conviction that the English king was a divine appointee, who was empowered to determine the doctrine of the church in his domain. But there were several who had a leaning towards Lutheranism. Archbishop Cranmer was one such appeaser. In 1532 he had spent several months in Germany (and even married clandestinely the daughter of a Lutheran theologian) and had come to embrace the doctrine of justification by faith which gave intellectual substance to the rejection of the church's reliance on penitential rituals. He was enthusiastically behind Cromwell's diplomatic overtures to the Protestant princes and to the Cleves match. It seems safe to assume that Catherine's stance was similar to that of the new archbishop, and, like his, it was still developing.

What those who occupied what we might call the "centre ground" of English Protestantism rejected was the two extremes of papalism and evangelical radicalism. It was in the mid-1530s that church leaders and magistrates began to be alarmed by the influx of "Anabaptism", a portmanteau term which embraced the "Reformed" theology of Huldrych Zwingli and other Swiss theologians, the violent, exclusivist teaching of "prophets" who set up communes in Germany and the Netherlands, and the ardent social revolutionism that launched the appalling Peasants' War of 1524–25 in Germany. "Anabaptism" thus meant for most people ideas disruptive of all law and order. Those who belonged to this frightening fringe tended to be identified by rejection of two central elements of sacramental theology – infant baptism and the mass. Members were accepted into their Anabaptist groups only by the initiation ceremony of adult baptism. As to the mass, what they denied was the corporal presence of Christ. Catholic dogma taught that when the celebrant repeated the words, "this is my body", "this is my blood", the elements on the altar actually changed. All evangelicals rejected the priestly miracle of the mass but they could not agree what to put in its place.

As early as 1529 the German and Swiss leaders had fallen out over their understanding of Christ's presence in the sacrament. In a debate at Marburg reform leaders from Wittenberg, Zurich, Basel, and Strasbourg reached agreement on fourteen out of fifteen points of doctrine, but on the Lord's Supper they were completely at loggerheads. Luther adhered to a literal understanding of the words "This is my body", but the Swiss theologians sought other ways to explain the mystery. Since even Christ could not be in two places at once, they insisted, he must have been talking figuratively. Over the years, arguments over what to modern ears seems like an arcane point had become heated and opinions ever more diverse. Was the sacrament a re-enactment or a memorial? Was Christ on the altar physically or spiritually? Was he only present by virtue of the faith of his people? Everyone believed in the centrality of the sacrament in the life of the church. They simply could not agree about what it meant.

In England, official teaching, like that of the Lutherans, had not moved very far from the Catholic position. Therefore, the bishops regarded all sacramentarians (that is, those who totally rejected the idea of a corporeal presence) as heretics and even worse than papists. Even Cranmer, at this time, was adamant that such

61

radicals should be made to recant and, if they persisted, handed over to the secular courts for condemnation and punishment.

The alarming fact was that, from about 1534, various kinds of radicalism were spreading, particularly in the south and east of England. There was a "ground base" of native heresy. Lollards had long cherished their founder's eucharistic teaching. From 1546, English radicals had at their disposal *Wycklyffes Wycket*, an exposition of sacramental theology based on illicit Lollard fragments now published in Nuremberg. John Wycliffe (or Wyclif), the fourteenth century instigator of what became known as 'Lollardy' or the 'English heresy' had insisted that the Lord's Supper was a remembrance "of the body of Christ, for a sacrament is no more to say but a sign of mind of a thing past."[33] To this was added, as we have seen, the works of Tyndale, smuggled in from abroad. There were Dutch and German beliefs disseminated along the trade routes from the eastern ports. There were foreign settlers (some fleeing from religious persecution). All of them were introducing their unsettling beliefs. And, to cap it all, there were vernacular gospels, read clandestinely before 1539 but openly thereafter. Readers who searched their Scriptures found there no reference to the priestly miracle of the mass. A plain, common-sense understanding of the biblical record suggested to many theologically unsophisticated people that what Jesus instituted on the eve of his Passion was a fellowship meal, a memorial, a symbolical aide-memoire that would bind his followers together and focus their minds and hearts on his sacrifice for them through the years and centuries to come.

But this was heresy and, as long as Henry VIII was alive, it would remain so. Anyone rejecting the miracle of the mass was tarred with the revolutionary brush, guilty of that damnable error, disseminated by those dangerous, anti-social, disruptive elements all lumped together as "Anabaptists". Since different tributaries spread into this rather muddy river it is, in many cases, difficult to identify the origins of unorthodox beliefs espoused by individuals.

There is no doubt that Anne Askew's religion was of an extremist hue. It is very likely that she was driven farther along the

---

33   Wycliffe J. *Wycklyffes Wycket*, 2012, p. 23.

heretical path by her unhappy domestic situation. Oral tradition claims that she had two children by Thomas Kyme. Bearing and rearing will have occupied much of her time and energy in the early years of her marriage but her zeal could not be muzzled and she believed she had a mission to go gospelling. The opposition of her husband and the local clergy only strengthened her resolve. The stress was intolerable. Anne decided not to tolerate it. Did not God's word tell true believers not to be "unequally yoked together with unbelievers"? Like other radicals she took Paul's injunction in I Corinthians 6:14 to heart. Sometime in the early 1540s she made good her escape from Friskney and sought refuge with her brother at South Kelsey. Now that her father was dead she might well feel that her brother would be more understanding of her plight.

For the next scene in what was becoming an intense drama we have to return to the royal court. And briefly occupying the position centre stage we find that member of the Privy Chamber staff, John Lascelles. In June 1541 Henry set out on his longest royal progress. He travelled by easy stages to York to show himself to the people of the unruly North, to satisfy himself of their loyalty and to show off his vivacious new queen. Lascelles was one of those not selected to be in the royal entourage. Freed from his chamber duties, he rode down into Sussex to spend some time with his sister Mary, now Mrs Hall. It is not clear whether sibling affection was his only motive for the visit or whether the zealous evangelical courtier had a clandestine, sinister motive. In any case, either by accident or design, John and his sister fell to discussing the "goings-on" of the young ladies in the Duchess of Norfolk's household, including the amorous adventures of Catherine Howard. There had been rumours about these things but Mary's brother pressed her for the truth.

Piece by piece, John assembled the chronicle of Catherine Howard's love affairs. At the age of fourteen she had held evening assignations in the Duchess's chamber with Henry Manox, her music teacher. This first sally into the excitements of love-play had not gone beyond intimate caresses. Of a different nature was the affair with Francis Dereham. Dereham, a gentleman attendant upon the Duke of Norfolk, took to visiting the girls' dormitory at night in company with other young gallants. They would bring with them "wine, strawberries, apples and other things to make good cheer" – prepared for nocturnal entertainment and the satisfying of more than one kind of appetite. The relationship between Catherine and Dereham soon developed into something more than amorous dalliance – certainly as far as the gentleman was concerned. He repeatedly asked his mistress to marry him but eventually had to accept the fact that no Howard girl was her own to give. At length Catherine was placed at court and Master Dereham's visits had to cease.

Henry, as everyone at court knew, was delirious about his spotless bride and proud of the sexual vigour she had aroused in him. There could be no doubt that he would find the truth humiliating. So what was John's motive in deciding to see that the facts reached the king? He was greatly distressed by the fall of his patron, Thomas Cromwell. More than that, he was disturbed that the movement towards reforming the English church might now be put into reverse. It was no secret that several bishops and leaders of secular society wanted to have the Great Bible withdrawn from circulation. A strategy was probably already in preparation for achieving this end by having Convocation and Parliament agree to set in hand a "revision" of the 1539 text which, in fact, would mean withdrawing the book while committees of bishops debated it line by line – a process that Cranmer sarcastically pointed out would keep them well occupied until doomsday. Back in September 1540, Lascelles had discussed these matters with fellow evangelicals in the royal court, one of whom reported that the Duke of Norfolk had declared his intention never to read the English Bible. Howard had been heard to grumble, "it was merry in England before the New Learning appeared." Lascelles and his colleagues had debated whether the duke could or should be reported for his open opposition to royal policy.[34] Nothing had come of this at the time, but Lascelles obviously continued to brood on the religious situation, doubtless earnestly praying for divine guidance as to whether and how to undermine the influence of the Howard clan. The removal of the queen and her relatives into the North on the

---

34   *L & P*, XVI, 101.

king's progress in late summer 1541 provided a good opportunity.

Having gathered the damning evidence against Queen Catherine, Lascelles had to decide what to do with it. It was no easy decision. If he revealed what he knew and was not believed, the consequences would be dire. He would face not only legal prosecution but might also be subject to a more rough-and-ready response from his powerful adversary. He would have been well advised to avoid unlit narrow streets. On the other hand, to suppress information detrimental to the king was a form of treason. It is very likely that Lascelles felt himself to be God's chosen agent, but it is certain that he was Henry's subject and, as such, his duty was clear. He laid his information in writing before Cranmer, who was likely to be the most sympathetic member of the London Council left in the capital. At his first opportunity after the king's return on 29 October the archbishop passed it on to Henry, who ordered the immediate discreet interrogation of John and his sister. When no holes could be poked in their story, a tearful king was forced to recognize that yet another of his wives had "failed" him.

Pre-marital sexual activity was just a crime and, if that was Catherine's only misdemeanour, she would have faced divorce and disgrace but nothing worse. However, when the royal "inquisition" got to work on the queen and her bedfellows, it became clear that she had commenced another affair with the courtier Thomas Culpepper after her marriage and for that there could be only one punishment.

Lascelles must have felt very satisfied with his work. From 12 November, when the scandal was made public, it seemed that the entire Howard family would fall under the royal displeasure. The Duke of Norfolk threw himself into a frenzy of activity directed against his niece and her lovers, hoping thereby to dissociate himself from their crimes. When he had done all he could, he prudently retired to his East Anglian estates. He was alone among the leading members of the family not to be arrested. Everyone connected with Catherine and her days at Horsham and Lambeth was sought out. All the ladies of the Duchess's household were questioned and some detained. The only exception made was for Mary Hall. The "Council with the King" at Greenwich specifically informed the "council in

London" that Mistress Hall was, "as an encouragement to others to reveal like cases, not to be troubled" – an instruction which the recipient considered "most graciously determined".[35]

On 13 February 1542, Catherine Howard was executed on Tower Green.

English political life between 1540 and 1546 has often been likened to a see-saw, with traditionalist and reformist factions constantly "up" or "down" in relation to each other. The succession of day and night might be a better metaphor. The reverses of fortune came about more gradually but also more inevitably. Changes of policy emanated from two power points, the Council and the Privy Chamber. This had always been the case but, now that the incapacitated king spent more time in his private apartments and seldom attended Council meetings, the few people who attended him on a daily basis exercised increased influence and were a counterbalance to the executive body. Cromwell had done his work well in promoting to the inner sanctum men of a reformist bent. Prominent among them were Sir William Butts, the royal physician, Anthony Denny, the Chief gentleman of the Privy Chamber, George Blagge, poet and close friend of Sir Thomas Wyatt, William Herbert, Catherine's brother-in-law, and William Parr, Catherine's brother. Some of these also attended Council meetings from time to time, though they were not political heavyweights. Those in this latter category who directly influenced policy and whom we may consider as progressives were Edward Seymour, Earl of Hertford, and John Dudley, Viscount Lisle (from 1542), both of whom owed much of their favour to long service as diplomats and military leaders.

While it is reasonable to see the political events of Henry's last years in terms of a faction feud, we must not lose sight of the fact that personal relations always counted for much with this king. He gave his favourites nicknames. George Blagge, for example, was "My Pig" and William Parr was dubbed "My Integrity", perhaps because he could get away with speaking his mind to the king. Personal affection counted for more than political (or theological)

---

35   *L & P*, XVI, 1340, 1343.

correctness with Henry. Humble submission usually achieved its objective. We shall see evidence of this more than once in the last five years of the reign.

Henry's initial reaction to any opposition was always defiance. This was true of the personal demons that now invaded his intimate life. He fought against his physical infirmity by partying, late-night gambling, and even by seeking military adventure. Nor did he allow his humiliation over being cuckolded by Catherine Howard to depress him for very long. On 29 January 1542, Eustace Chapuys reported that his majesty had given a great supper for sixty-one ladies – twenty-six at his own table and thirty-five at an adjacent board. The ambassador identified two ladies as having engaged Henry's particular attention. Anne Basset was someone he had long felt affection for. The other was Elizabeth Brooke. This was, almost certainly, William Parr's longstanding mistress (whom he would eventually marry).

Was William's sister, Lady Latimer, among this company? It is possible. Her husband was in London early in the year in order to attend Parliament before being sent north yet again to help in the war that had broken out with Scotland. The frequent to-ing and fro-ing between the capital and the northern border took their toll on Lord Latimer and in February 1543 he died. He was only half way through his fiftieth year. On 2 March he was accorded a funeral in St Paul's Cathedral befitting his status.

Four months later, Catherine wrote to William Parr, who was still serving in the North:

> Right dear and well-beloved brother, we greet you well.
> Letting you wit that where it hath pleased almighty God
> of His goodness to incline the King's majesty in such wise
> towards me, as it hath pleased his highness to take me
> of all others, most unworthy, to his wife, which is, as of
> reason it ought to be, the greatest joy and comfort that
> could happen to me in this world.
>
> To the intent, you being my natural brother, may rejoice
> with me in the goodness of God and of his majesty, as

the person who by nature hath most cause of the same, I thought meet to give you this advertisement. And to require you to let me sometime hear of your health as friendly as you would have done, if God and his majesty had not called me to this honor: which, I assure you, shall be much to my comfort.[36]

The feelings Catherine expressed in this letter were not how she remembered them and described them four years later when writing to another man:

I would not have you to think that this mine honest goodwill toward you to proceed of any sudden motion or passion. For, as truly as God is God, my mind was fully bent the other time I was at liberty, to marry you before any man I knew. Howbeit, God withstood my will therein most vehemently for a time and, through His grace and goodness, made that possible which seemeth to me most unpossible that was, made me to renounce utterly mine own will, and to follow His will most willingly. It were too long to write all the process of this matter. If I live, I shall declare it to you myself. I can say nothing but, as my lady of Suffolk saith, "God is a marvellous man."

By her that is yours to serve and obey during her life,

Katherine the Queen KP[37]

In the summer of 1543, one of our leading ladies was desperately trying to escape from a marriage. The other was confronting the realities of a new marriage with mixed feelings. From this point their stories converged and took centre stage in the story of England.

---

36   Mueller J. (ed.) *Katherine Parr – Complete Works and Correspondence*, Chicago, 2011, p. 46.
37   Mueller 2011, p. 131.

PART 2

The Crisis

CHAPTER 6

Thunder Round the Throne

Who list his wealth and ease retain,
Himself let him unknown contain.
Press not too fast in at that gate
Where the return stands by disdain,
For sure, circa Regna tonat [it thunders round the throne]

S ir Thomas Wyatt's well-known poem related his reaction to the events surrounding the fall of Anne Boleyn in 1536, but life in the royal court was no less hazardous six years later. The background to the events of the next few years is darkly tinged with apprehension. Few people could remember a national life not dominated by the super ego of Henry VIII. Whether one admired or loathed this king, whether one resented or welcomed the changes he had forced on the nation, whether one belonged to the fashionable courtly elite or lived in provincial obscurity, one could not deny the fact that Henry VIII had given England strong government. But now Henry was ailing and (although no one dared to breathe the sober truth) the probability was that he would not live to see his heir reach his majority. Who, then, would hold the country together and enable it to resist any counterattack launched by a vengeful papacy?

At the centre of national life, progressive and traditionalist activists took every opportunity to shape the future. In March 1542, Cranmer adroitly saw off a conservative attack on the 1539 Bible but, to quote the words of the Duke of Wellington about the Battle of Waterloo, it was "a damned nice thing – the nearest run thing you ever saw". The debate in Convocation on "Cromwell's Bible" was "one of the most disrupted and rowdy of the century".[38] Gardiner and his associates were intent on torpedoing the very concept of vernacular Scripture. In a letter a few years later, the Bishop of Winchester revealed his conviction that the mere idea of a "people's Bible" was socially and politically disruptive:

> ... if we are persuaded that the understanding of God's law is [granted to] women and children, whereby they may have control of it [it follows] that God's law must be controlled by all, and is not hereby all authority brought into their hands?[39]

Convocation agreed that printing of the Great Bible should be halted pending a wholesale revision by the bishops. Cranmer outmanoeuvred his colleagues by going over their heads. The king, he informed them, had decreed that the work of revision should be taken out of their hands and handed over to the universities (which would, of course, take for ever). The conservatives hit back, complaining in Parliament about the growing public debate to which the open Bible was giving rise and trying, without success, to ban all books on religion in English. Gardiner and others did not give up. Taking advantage of the king's hatred of heresy and desire for unity, they set in motion a revision of official doctrine which appeared in 1543 under the title *The Necessary Doctrine and Erudition for Any Christian Man*, commonly known as the *King's Book* (because Henry had a close interest in its production). In May 1543, they also achieved the passage through Parliament of the Act for the Advancement of True Religion. This was an attempt to lessen the impact of the English Bible. Its enemies could not demand its wholesale confiscation and burning. That would have been far too embarrassing for the government. What they could do – or naively thought they could do – was stop people reading it. This piece of legislation forbade all women, all servants, all dependent relatives

---

38   MacCulloch D. *Thomas Cranmer: A Life*, London, 1996, p. 289.
39   Muller J. (ed.) *The Letters of Stephen Gardiner*, Cambridge, 1933, p. 293.

and all male householders below the rank of yeoman to read the Bible. Thanks to a last-minute protest, ladies of noble or gentry stock were excluded from the ban. This tool fashioned by the leaders of reaction was intended for use against humble gospellers and simple people who gathered with their neighbours to read and discuss Scripture but its social implications were not so strictly defined. Some heretic networks were extensive and a strand once discovered might lead to quite exalted victims. Those determined to arrest what they saw as the slide into anarchy and unbelief were prepared to use any and every means to stop the "rot" which was spreading from the top down. Therefore, the possibility of a sixth royal marriage, bringing with it intimate access to the monarch by the bride's family was of interest to all concerned.

The imperial ambassador Chapuys, closely observing Henry VIII's moods, detected a significant change towards the end of 1542. He had ordered his daughter Mary to come to court for Christmas, attended by several ladies. Noting the elaborate preparations in hand at Hampton Court, the ambassador speculated, "it is possible that amid these festivities, the King might think of remarrying, although there is yet no bruit of it." Henry was feeling the need for a wife and the eligible women of Princess Mary's entourage were, doubtless, being urged to catch his eye. It seems unlikely that Catherine was among them. Her husband was once more back in London but was too ill to attend Parliament. She would hardly have abandoned him over Christmas. While the king entertained his female guests and considered his options, Lady Latimer did her wifely duty.

Lord Latimer's death a few weeks later changed everything. What inclined Henry to seek the new widow's hand? Probably that calm acceptance of duty she was demonstrating. He had had his fill of meddlesome beauties and also of foreign princesses. Catherine was still young and attractive, and combined with these attributes had maturity and intelligence. The king was also well disposed towards the Parr family. Anne had risen to become senior woman of the chamber to both of the recent queens and William was Captain of the ceremonial guard of Gentleman Pensioners. Both Catherine's siblings had become prominent and dependable members of the royal entourage.

Yet there remains one other factor that may have inclined Henry towards Catherine. Competition. There was a rival bidding for Lady Latimer's affections. Thomas Seymour was thirty-five (six years older than Catherine), the younger of Prince Edward's two uncles and thus very close to the throne. He was personable, extrovert, and confident in his own ability – the sort of person to whom others, especially women, are readily attracted. He made overtures to Catherine and she warmly responded. Their mutual attraction must have predated Latimer's demise, but Catherine behaved circumspectly and there was no hint of scandal. Once she was free, there must have been talk around the court of an impending marriage. That would have been enough to ignite the king's interest. It is unlikely to have been a coincidence that, within a few days of Latimer's funeral in March 1543, Seymour was appointed as ambassador to the Spanish Netherlands and service abroad kept him out of the realm for most of the remainder of Henry's reign. Sometime in the next few weeks Henry proposed.

Catherine's response was a game-changer, the importance of which has seldom been recognized. It would be an exaggeration to say that the Reformation hung upon it, but Lady Latimer certainly held in her hands the destiny of England. An enormous amount depended upon her response – for her, her family, her friends, and all who shared her religious convictions. She agonized in prayer over her response. There was no exaggeration in her claim that, "God withstood my will therein most vehemently for a time". She knew that she was undergoing strong temptation. But wherein lay that temptation? Was it the lusts of the flesh that sought to drag her down? She was in love with Seymour and longed to give him more than her heart. She was a woman of many passions, as her letters and devotional writings testify. In them we read anger, jealousy, and indignation, as well as kindness, thoughtfulness, and a strong sense of duty. She also loved fine clothes. An extant copy of a portrait dating from around the time of her third marriage shows her in a very expensive, heavily embroidered gown, studded with pearls and Tudor roses in gold thread. Surviving bills reveal her interest in dress and in perfumes for herself and her bedchamber. Here was no prudish, evangelical bluestocking. Catherine was a red-blooded woman who longed for the true love of a husband who could give her children. She must have asked whether God really wanted her to devote what remained of her best years to yet another older, semi-invalid spouse. Was it fleshly appetites that were tempting her? In which case, one word would banish it – "Yes". Or was it pride? She was being offered the highest position in the realm that could be bestowed on a woman. Wealth and the adulation of the people would be hers. To conquer this temptation she only had to say "No".

It would be interesting to know whether Catherine had any inkling of what was on the king's mind or whether it came as a bolt from the blue. She, at least, had the presence of mind to ask for time to consider her answer. It is not difficult to guess what some of her principal concerns must have been.

Family considerations will have weighed heavily with her. It was within Catherine's power to make the Parrs the second dynasty in the land. On St George's Day (23 April) brother William's name was added to the select list of Knights of the Garter. Days later, he was appointed Lord Warden and Keeper of the Western March, responsible for law and order on part of the border. Catherine's brother-in-law William Herbert was knighted and received lands in Wales which enabled him to begin work on a magnificent country residence, Wilton House, near Salisbury. Were these far-from-subtle hints that the king could make (or break) the Parrs and their kin?

As she probed the mind of God, however, Catherine sought to discern what deeper issues might be at stake in her elevation to the position of royal consort. The kind of reflection that might have swayed her is indicated by a letter she received in her early days as queen. It was from Francis Goldsmith, one of several evangelicals who sought placement in Catherine's entourage. Like all requests for patronage, it was effulgent in its praise of the recipient:

> If the most pious Queen Esther, consumed by zeal of the house of God and His glory, will never suffer the glory of her name to be blotted out, especially among the saints, because she ever most eagerly cherished nothing more important or illustrious than that the Israelite people, hard

pressed by the harsh servitude under which they had been put, should go free.

By how much more the name of your excellency, most noble Queen, will leave its traces ... By as much as Christ is greater than Solomon; by as much as the wisdom of the former abounds over that of the latter; by how much more steadfast and more sufficient learning is, freeing the people of God from the tyranny of the devil to strive with all their might and exert themselves; by how much they suffer in the flesh towards the things to come; by so much more your praise in the kingdom of God will doubtless be sustained by the mightier fruits that you bring forth.[40,41]

This will not have been the first time that Catherine had heard herself compared to Esther, the Jewish queen of the fifth–sixth-century BC Persian King Ahasuerus who used her position to protect her people from persecution (as recorded in the Old Testament book bearing her name). In seeking to discover God's will she must have asked herself the question that had been asked of Esther, "who knoweth whether thou art come to the kingdom for such a time as this?" (Esther 4:14). It may be that Catherine also discussed her big decision with her closest friends at court, women who shared her convictions. As well as her sister Anne Herbert, members of the inner circle included Lady Hertford, Lady Lisle, Lady Sussex, and the Duchess of Suffolk.

All of them were committed to reform and Lady Suffolk was a particularly outspoken and zealous champion of the Gospel who, during the reign of Mary Tudor, chose exile in preference to life under a Catholic regime. She was open in her contempt for the agents of reaction and caused much laughter around the court by

---

40   Mueller J. (ed.) *Katherine Parr – Complete Works and Correspondence*, Chicago, 2011, p. 77.

41   Goldsmith's suit was successful. He entered the queen's household, became a Member of Parliament, and ended his days as a staunch upholder of the Protestant establishment under Elizabeth I.

calling her pet spaniel "Gardiner". Anne Radcliffe, Countess of Sussex, was another Marian refugee and would later be estranged from her husband because of her religious beliefs. Lady Hertford and Lady Lisle were the wives of Henry's favourite warrior-councillors, Edward Seymour and John Dudley, both of whom enjoyed special prominence because, in his later years, King Henry once more went to war with Scotland and France.

Catherine's was a hard decision. When she turned to her Bible for guidance, she found in Paul's epistle to the Romans a very clear endorsement of temporal authority: "There is no power, but of God; the existing rulers are ordained by God. So, whoever resists such rulers, resists the will of God" (Romans 13:1–2). It was to this delegated authority that Catherine finally bowed and was able to "renounce utterly mine own will and follow [God's] will most willingly". Her "yes" to Henry revealed both her devotion and her strength of character. She resigned herself to estrangement from Thomas Seymour, knowing full well that, after the debacle of the Howard marriage there would have to be a permanent distancing from the man she loved.

The question must, of course, be asked whether Catherine really had any choice. Could she have turned the king down without dire consequences for herself and her family? Henry's advances had been spurned at least once before. Christina of Denmark had famously responded that if she had a spare head she would be happy to put it at the King of England's disposal. But she, of course, was a foreign princess and quite safe from any repercussions. Henry was not familiar with the word "no", but he was also gallant enough to recognize that a woman needs to be courted rather than commanded. His surviving letters to Anne Boleyn reveal a man fully conversant with the rules of the love game. It is unlikely that he would have "punished" Catherine for her refusal. But consequences there most certainly would have been. The choice facing Catherine was a stark one: Influence or Oblivion – for her and her family. So much of her life had been involved with the royal court and she could now become the second person in that court, with all the opportunities this would afford her, through the patronage network, to advance the beliefs she held and the people she approved of. The alternative would have been, in effect, banishment to the provinces and also the door left open for some other consort proposed by the enemies of reform. This, I think, must have been the clincher for her. Henry and Catherine were married in a quiet, private ceremony in a chapel at Hampton Court on 12 July 1543.

This event was significant for another reason. The celebrant who joined the bride and groom in wedlock was not, as might have been expected, the Archbishop of Canterbury. It was the primate's determined enemy, Bishop Gardiner of Winchester, the man who was rumoured to have said that he would give £6,000 to pluck down the archbishop. Cranmer was under a cloud – or, rather, a whole stack of storm clouds whipped up by the forces of reaction. There was a determined and prolonged effort by Gardiner and his clientage to neutralize the influence of evangelicals at court and Cranmer was their prime target. Throughout 1543, vigorous activity was centred on Windsor and Canterbury (and throughout much of Kent). The basic formula was so well tried as to be almost a convention. Minor suspects were picked up, imprisoned, and accused of heresy. They were interrogated, often under torture, in order to induce them to recant, but also to prove their sincere return to the Catholic fold by naming others of their "cell" among their social superiors, who, in their turn, were also examined. The intention was always that using humble "sprats" might lead to the netting of some pretty big mackerel.

Two weeks after the wedding, a heresy trial took place in Windsor. Three of the accused were local townsmen but the others were members of the Chapel Royal and their accusers hoped, through them, to reach members of the king's inner circle. The campaign had begun early in the year, its prime mover being Dr John London, Warden of New College, Oxford, one of the most odious creatures who tried to turn the troubles of these years to his own advantage. He began his career of "professional persecutor" as a monastic visitor serving Cromwell's regime and was notorious for bullying monks and – especially – nuns. After Cromwell's fall, London was quick to shift his allegiance to Bishop Gardiner and devote his skills to sniffing out offenders against the Act of Six Articles. In March, he laid information against associates of a

Sacramentarian preacher at Windsor, among whom were members of the Chapel Royal, as well as a group of courtiers, including Sir Philip Hoby, Sir Thomas Caradine, Sir Thomas Weldon, the king's barber, Edmund Harmon, and Cranmer's friend, Simon Haynes, Dean of Exeter. As a result, Hoby and Haynes were sent to the Fleet prison. But Henry was not prepared to allow any members of his chamber staff to go to the flames for heresy. After a few days he ordered the prisoners' release.

Humbler men were not so fortunate. Among the lesser fry of the "Windsor Martyrs" were two members of the Chapel Royal, the organist and composer John Marbeck, and Robert Testwood, a singing man. Testwood was certainly a provocative and argumentative evangelical, but Marbeck consistently denied any radical leanings. It may well have been because the latter was weak and easily frightened that he was subjected to weeks of cruel and persistent interrogation, some of it by Gardiner in person. Marbeck's tormentors resorted to both threats and bribes in their efforts to induce him to give false evidence against Hoby, Haynes, and others but the musician's integrity held firm:

> Whereas your lordship will have me to write such things as I know of my fellows at home, pleaseth it your lordship to understand that I cannot call to remembrance any manner of thing whereby I might justly accuse any one of them, unless it be that the reading of the New Testament, which is common to all men, be an offence: more than this I know not.[42]

The conclusion of the Windsor purge came on 28 July, when three of the radicals were burned to death. Gardiner personally obtained a pardon for Marbeck. It would be pleasant to think that he had been moved by the musician's courage and transparent honesty.

All this time a wide-ranging heresy hunt had been under way in Cranmer's own diocese of Canterbury. Evangelical preachers

---

42   Redworth G. *In Defence of the Church Catholic: The Life of Stephen Gardiner*, Oxford, 1990, p. 193.

with the archbishop's licence were touring Kent and were bitterly resented by their conservative enemies. The cathedral staff were divided between pro- and anti-Cranmer lobbies. One of the senior clergy there was Germain Gardiner, the bishop's nephew, and he was the main contact between the Kentish malcontents and the royal Council. It was he who provided Winchester with a list of complaints about the archbishop which were passed on to the king. This was why Cranmer was under a cloud around the time of the royal wedding.

But Gardiner and his supporters had overreached themselves. Henry recalled how he had been inveigled into getting rid of Cromwell, only to regret it bitterly. He was not going to divest himself of the archbishop who, whatever his religious convictions, had served him unwaveringly for more than a decade. There was also the war effort to take into account. The king was planning a major military expedition to France. To have executed his primate would have been a diplomatic own goal at a time when national unity was of particular importance. The martyrologist John Foxe recorded how Henry dealt with this particular dilemma. In a confidential meeting with Cranmer, he revealed the complaints being made about the maladministration of the diocese and instructed him to deal with the problem in person. The defendant was made judge and jury. Cranmer's commissioners did their work thoroughly. But now it was the traditionalist troublemakers who fell under the spotlight. Night raids on suspects discovered incriminating letters between ringleaders at the centre of power and their rural minions. Some threw themselves on Cranmer's mercy but Gardiner and his close advisers decided that the best form of defence was attack. They gathered their best evidence against the archbishop and presented it to the king, who granted permission for Cranmer to be called before the Council to face heresy charges. This determined and vehement clash between Catholic and evangelical forces at the very centre of English life reveals dramatically and vividly what was at stake in a confrontation which, to our secular age, may seem esoteric, a conflict between rival theologies. Not so: this was a life-and-death struggle for the soul of England.

Henry was determined to defuse the situation. While permitting the examination of his archbishop, he organized a piece of theatre to stop it. He summoned Cranmer for a nocturnal meeting, told him of the plot, and gave him his ring as a token of his royal protection. The archbishop duly obeyed the conciliar summons and, after being kept waiting for the best part of an hour, was informed by his erstwhile colleagues that he was under arrest. It was a re-run of the event that had initiated Cromwell's destruction. Almost. Cranmer produced Henry's ring and the opposition collapsed in total confusion. The coda to these traumatic events came in the early weeks of 1544. Germain Gardiner was executed for treason and Dr London died in prison where he had been incarcerated for perjury.

King Henry by now had other ideas on his mind – grander, more expansive and vastly more expensive ideas. After an interval of seventeen years he decided to go to war again. He launched campaigns against both of England's traditional enemies: France and Scotland. This was no sudden impulse. Henry had been systematically improving the coastal defences and modernizing the navy. In 1543 he bound himself to launching a joint attack on France with Spain's King Charles V. The king decided to lead this expedition himself. But the Scots insisted on complicating his plans. At the end of the year they made a new pact with France. Henry responded by appointing Edward Seymour lieutenant-general in the North with instructions to carry out savage reprisals which merely served to strengthen pro-French feelings in Scotland. The border, however, was secure for the time being and, on the anniversary of his marriage to Catherine, Henry was able to set out across the Channel to join his army, leaving his queen in charge of the government of England.

CHAPTER 7

Divorce

Under what circumstances may a Christian husband or wife seek to terminate a marriage? That was the question that lay at the heart of England's Reformation. Henry VIII desperately explored Scripture, Church tradition and canon law in his attempt to legitimize setting aside Catherine of Aragon. But kings were not alone in experiencing marital problems to which escape seemed the only answer. The rule of the church was clear: marriage was for life and anyone seeking to break that bond committed sin. However, the divisions in society created by the Reformation put a strain on some unions and many converts to evangelical faith took a leaf from their sovereign's book in resorting to the Bible in search of support for leaving a spouse of contrary religious convictions. Anne Askew turned to 1 Corinthians to find justification for escaping from her forced and miserable marriage.

The Apostle Paul had set forth his opinion quite clearly (1 Corinthians 7:12–15 [GNB]), while pointing out that it was just that – an opinion – and not a dominical command:

> … I say (I, myself, not the Lord): if a Christian man has a wife who is an unbeliever and she agrees to go on living with him, he must not divorce her. And if a Christian woman is married to a man who is an unbeliever and he agrees to go on living with her, she must not divorce him. For the unbelieving husband is made acceptable to God by being united to his wife, and the unbelieving wife is made acceptable to God by being united to her Christian

husband … However, if the one who is not a believer wishes to leave the Christian partner, whether husband or wife, let it be so. In such cases the Christian partner, whether husband or wife, is free to act.

How far these words applied to the Kyme household is not clear. One reading of the evidence suggests that Anne walked away from the marriage, but another states that Thomas Kyme threw his wife out. What is clear is that Anne left Friskney – probably sometime in 1543 – and sought the protection of her brother at South Kelsey. Francis Askew was sympathetic (though, doubtless, embarrassed by the situation).

Back in familiar surroundings and enjoying the company of her brother, his wife, and their young family, Anne was able to enjoy a few months of peace. But it could not last. She was anxious to make her separation from Kyme permanent and Francis, despite all his concern for his sister, would also have wanted a resolution to the awkward situation in which he had been placed. The only place where Anne's appeal for a divorce could be heard was in the bishop's court at Lincoln. So, to Lincoln she went.

In her later writings Anne made no mention of a legal case and there are no extant records. She must have been unsuccessful and nor should we expect otherwise. The episcopal lawyers would not have been disposed to be lectured on scriptural exegesis by a mere woman. Also, by now she had achieved more than a little notoriety, as she wrote later:

> … my friends told me, if I did come to Lincoln, the priests would assault me and put me to great trouble, as thereof they had made their boast. And when I heard it, I went thither indeed, not being afraid, because I knew my matter to be good. Moreover, I remained there nine days, to see what would be said unto me. And as I was in the Minster reading upon the Bible, they resorted unto me by two and by two, by five and by six, minding to have spoken unto me, yet went their ways again without words speaking …

there was one of them at the last which did speak to me
indeed … his words were of small effect …[43]

Her biographer asserted shortly after her death that there were
threescore priests at Lincoln "bent against her".[44] Anne's quiet
defence would have been extremely frustrating for the clergy. Here
was a member of one of the leading county families reading the
Great Bible which had royal approval. There was no law they could
cite against her. She was not preaching anything contrary to the
Act of Six Articles and she was not in contravention of the Act
for the Advancement of True Religion. That statute had exempted
ladies of noble or gentry status, who were permitted to read the
Bible for their own edification. Mistress Kyme was becoming a
thorn in the flesh for which there appeared to be no remedy.

From this point it is difficult to be sure of the precise sequence
of events. However, it seems likely that Anne's next move occurred
in the summer of 1544. It was then that Francis Askew set off for
France as a captain in the king's invading army. Without her defender,
South Kelsey would no longer be a safe haven. It was decided that
Anne should go to London. There she had friends and family in
high places. Her brother, Christopher, had recently died (perhaps
of the plague which visited the capital in the autumn of 1543) but
her older brother, Edward, had been promoted from Cranmer's
household to that of the king and was on the Privy Chamber staff
as a cup-bearer. There was also a cousin, Christopher Brittayne, of
the Middle Temple, who obviously had a great deal of influence
and who later went to considerable lengths to extricate her from
trouble. In addition, there were Anne's contacts among the East
Midlands gentry we have encountered before. Foremost among
them was John Lascelles. According to Anne's biographer, he was
her "instructor".[45] It is tantalizing that we know nothing more
about this relationship and particularly whether or not it predated
Anne's arrival in London. Anne's friends and supporters among

---

43   Bale J. *Select Works* (ed. H. Christmas), Cambridge, 1849, pp. 173–74.
44   Bale 1849, pp. 173–74.
45   Beilin E. V. (ed.) *The Examinations of Anne Askew*, Oxford, 1996, p. 154.

the legal fraternity included the historian Edward Hall. We can, however, safely assume that Anne had access to the royal court, a court now presided over by Queen Catherine.

As she arrived in the centre of national life, what did she discover? All the evidence suggests that London in the second half of 1544 was confused, depressed, and angry, a city astir with fears, rumours, and resentments. There were three major reasons for the widespread discontent. An underlying cause and one which no one understood was inflation. Between 1526 and 1546 householders experienced a fifty per cent rise in the cost of living – and that at a time when wages were static. On top of this basic economic dislocation came the king's unpopular French war and the means employed to finance it. Direct taxation took various forms – forced loans, benevolences (that is, forced "gifts") and subsidies. In a desperate attempt to fill the gap between receipts and expenditure on foreign mercenaries, war materiel, naval expansion, and new coastal defences, the government resorted to debasing the coinage and selling off quickly what remained of ex-monastic property (which reduced the value of land generally). The Lord Chancellor, Thomas Wriothesley, was at his wits' end to make ends meet:

> ... touching the Mint we be now so far out with that,
> if you take any penny more from it these three months
> ... you shall utterly destroy the trade of it ... as to the
> Augmentations it shall not be able to pay the £5,000 ...
> yet these six days ... And of the revenue ... there is yet to
> come in ... £15,000 or £16,000, but when we shall have it,
> God knoweth. As to the Tenth and Firstfruits, there remains
> not due about £10–12,000, which is not payable till after
> Christmas ... The Exchequer shall not be able to minister
> about £10,000 (and that at Candlemass) of the remainder of
> the subsidy. The Surveyors Court owes so much that when
> all shall be come in that is due to it ... they shall not be able
> to render up ... more than £5,000 or £6,000; and when that
> shall be, God knoweth. So that, if you tarry for more money
> to be sent to Boulogne at this time, you may perhaps tarry
> too long, before you have the sum desired ... I assure you,

Master Secretary, I am at my wits' end how we shall possibly shift for three months following, and especially for the next two. For I see not any great likelihood, that any good sum will come in till after Christmas.[46]

The general despair in government circles was summed up by Bishop Gardiner in a letter to Secretary, William Paget:

We are at war with France and Scotland, we have enmity with the bishop of Rome, we have no assured friendship … with the Emperor and we have received from the Landgrave [of Hesse], chief captain of the Protestants, such displeasure that he has cause to think us angry with him … Our war is noisome to our realm and to all our merchants that traffic through the Narrow Seas … We are in a world where reason and learning prevail not and covenants are little regarded.[47]

So councillors grumbled among themselves but, of course, did not dare to voice their concerns to the king.

They shared the views of most ordinary citizens. Gardiner was right when he spoke of the war as being noisome to our realm. When a visitor, such as Anne Askew, wandered the market stalls of Cheapside she would have seen how grudgingly buyers and sellers handled the new debased coins. In the taverns she would have heard men grumbling about the government's financial exactions. She might have heard the story of a prominent citizen who had refused to pay the latest levy. When this "effrontery" was reported to the king, he flew into a rage and ordered the poor man to be sent to join the army in Scotland, where he did not long survive. But it was not just financial exactions that angered people. There were other grievances. Enormous numbers of the realm's able-bodied men were away on military service. At the turn of the year,

---

46   *L & P*, I, pt. ii, 840.
47   Muller J. (ed.) *The Letters of Stephen Gardiner*, Cambridge, 1933, pp. 185 and 198.

besides the army in France, there was another on the Scottish border, the coasts were guarded by forces in Essex, Devon, and Kent, and Lord Admiral Dudley was at sea with twelve thousand troops. In all over sixty thousand men were under arms. Food was another problem. Large quantities of grain and meat had to be commandeered for the army and this left the civilian populations to face short supplies and rising prices. London even had to import grain from the Continent. But more disturbing to the citizenry than all these privations was the threat of invasion. The southern coasts were put in a state of readiness and English agents kept a close watch on the French fleet, wondering not if but when to expect an enemy counterattack.

The general disaffection could not avoid impacting on the religious conflict. Murmuring against the status quo was directed against those in authority, whether spiritual or temporal. Wriothesley found himself under personal attack for being zealous in his hostility to evangelicals, as he complained to Paget:

> Master Secretary, I send unto you herewith a bill [a note] which was let fall yesterday, as I was going to mass, in my dining chamber. I pray you show it to His Highness and discover his pleasure, what he would should be done about it. You know that when those naughty books were brought unto me, I could do not less than send them to His Highness, and also labour, as much as I could, to find out the author; wherein, that I have not much prevailed, yet some people be angry with my doing. Upon your answer of His Majesty's pleasure, I shall do as the same shall command me. I pray you return the bill again to me.[48]

In the middle of 1544 a majority in the House of Commons pushed through Parliament a modification of the Act of Six Articles. It excluded from prosecution all alleged offences more than a year old and stated that no sermons could be challenged after forty days had passed. This seems to have encouraged a

---

48   *L & P*, I, pt. ii, 840.

fresh outbreak of evangelical preaching. Hugh Latimer and Nicholas Shaxton, two bishops who had resigned over the Act of Six Articles, were now openly active in city pulpits and were received among the queen's circle at court. Edward Crome was again gathering fashionable congregations at St Mary Aldermary. At St Bride's in Fleet Street, the vicar, John Cardmaker (alias Taylor), was attracting eager listeners to his unorthodox doctrine of the mass and his occasional attacks on Gardiner and Bonner. At St Catherine Coleman a fiery Scot, William Whitehead, was one of many outspoken priests and friars who had been forced to flee across the border by persecution in his native land. But licensed preachers were not the only – and, indeed, not the main – exponents of religious novelties in London. Throughout the city there were many groups meeting, some in secret, others more openly, for Bible study and discussion. Preoccupation with the war and the control of the court by the queen and her evangelical friends weakened any Catholic reaction in the short term and, from November 1544, Gardiner was absent on an embassy to the emperor. It seems, then, that Anne arrived in London at a comparatively safe time for outspoken radicals.

She took lodgings near the Temple, which provided easy access to Westminster and to the inns of court, places where she had trusted friends. If John Lascelles was her guide to the religious life of court and capital he will have been able to introduce her to the more exciting preachers and teachers in London and also to the members of the queen's entourage. Anne will have been courteously received by Lady Suffolk, Lady Herbert, Lady Hertford, and Lady Lisle; and, perhaps, by Catherine herself. Two years later, her enemies were confident of being able to connect the "fair gospeller" to the queen and her inner circle but they were never able to produce evidence in support of their suspicions. This suggests that Anne was not as intimate with Queen Catherine as romantic legends have liked to suggest. As regent, Catherine was, of course, very busy. She may also have been cautious. Anne seems to have become something of a celebrity in the world of London's religious radicals and her views were more extreme than Catherine's. It would have been unwise to be seen as openly offering patronage.

This does not mean that the two ladies in our story never met; merely that we have no evidence for such a meeting.

From Lascelles and the bolder spirits to whom he introduced her, Anne learned more extreme views than those she had held previously. She arrived in London as a Bible student with a remarkable knowledge of the Scriptures but now she encountered believers who were grappling with complex theological issues. In the mid-1540s all thinking evangelicals, throughout Europe, were debating those points of doctrine on which they differed from Rome and, in some instances, on which they differed from one another. The thorniest issue was the eucharistic one: what actually happens in the communion service at the moment of consecration? The leading Continental reformers had failed to reach agreement on this. We know that Archbishop Cranmer, himself, changed his stance on it during these years and for heresy hunters the doctrine of the mass came to be the litmus test used to identify orthodox believers as distinct from those outcasts frequently lumped together as "Anabaptists". The difficulty for the ardent Bible believer was that Jesus had said, quite specifically, "this is my body ... this is my blood", but Catholics had used this as the basis of the "priestly miracle" which endowed the celebrant with mystical (seemingly magical) powers to actually effect change in the elements. How could one reject the latter, while yet retaining the essential truth of the former? Without delving into philosophical complexities inappropriate in the present context, what we can say is that an increasing number of evangelicals were coming to regard the eucharistic elements as "signs" or "symbols". A sign is a thing which signifies another thing. Thus, while bread and wine remained bread and wine, they signified Christ's presence at the service. John Lascelles explained his position in a letter of 1546:

> ... where the bread is broken according to the ordinance of Christ, the blessed and immaculate Lamb is present to the eyes of our faith, and so we eat his flesh and drink his blood, which is, to dwell with God and God with us ...
> In this I do differ from the pope's church, that the priests

have authority to make Christ's natural presence in the bread, for so doth he more than our Lord and Saviour did …[49]

In the absence of any other evidence we may assume that this is the position Anne Askew came to hold.

For the best part of a year she lived, trouble free, in her new environment. It is not difficult to imagine how much she must have enjoyed her life in London after her stressful recent experiences in Lincolnshire. As well as the bustle of the city and the refined life of the court, she enjoyed fellowship with others who shared her faith. Among them she soon became something of a celebrity. Nor is it difficult to see why. Hers was a lively and forthright personality. For all her fine clothes, her education, and her breeding, she was one who had "suffered for righteousness' sake" and this made her something of a "darling" among the Protestants. She earned the respect of many for her monumental knowledge of the Bible. There was scarcely a topic of conversation on which she could not quote some relevant proof text. She knew the articles of her faith backwards and was unassailable in argument. But she was not solemn and unsmiling with it all; she had a ready wit and her arguments were spiced with jokes and jibes – not always kind, but always lively. Nor was she frightened to confront anyone; priests, bishops, canon lawyers, doctors of theology, she would express her opinions before all of them, in complete assurance that the truth must prevail. And she was not any respecter of persons: her pert answers to adversaries and her rude jibes about Catholic leaders were soon being joked about in the city taverns. One could like or loathe Anne Askew. What one could not do was ignore her.

Anne's new way of life among her wide circle of friends and acquaintances passed uneventfully until the spring of 1545. But by then she had come to the attention of the authorities and made enemies who were prepared to accuse her of heresy. As a result she and two other members of her group, Joan Sawtry, wife of a London merchant, and Thomas Lukine, servant to Sir Humphrey Brown

---

49   Foxe J. *Acts and Monuments*, Volume V, p. 552.

(a justice of the King's Bench), were arrested by the Six Articles commissioners in March and presented for preliminary trial by the "quest" at the Guildhall on 13 June.[50] Since the modified legislation of 1544, all suspects of heresy were required to be condemned by a jury of twelve before they could be committed to prison to await further examination. Accordingly the three were presented at the Guildhall "for certain words spoken by them against the sacrament". But the trial turned out to be something of a farce. No witness appeared to testify against the two women and the evidence presented against Lukine was considered suspect. Thus the trio were found not guilty by "twelve honest and substantial men of the city of London" and released.[51]

However, Anne still had her marital problem to sort out. It seems that one reason for travelling to London was to pursue her divorce claim in the court of Chancery. This might help to explain her long sojourn in the city. Getting a plea heard and then considered was a long-drawn-out business requiring great patience on the part of all concerned. One of the twenty-four cursitors in Chancery (the clerks who drafted writs) was a certain Master Wadloe. He now took an interest in Anne and obtained lodgings close to hers in order to spy on her. Whether he was acting on his own initiative or as an agent for Lord Chancellor Wriothesley is not clear. According to the chronicler John Strype, Wadloe was "hot in his religion and thinking not well of her life".[52] One reason for the surveillance was to discover who visited her. This suggests that Wadloe's activity was part of a more comprehensive strategy initiated from above. Wriothesley certainly developed an interest in Anne's connections and it may well be that that interest started now. The conservative leadership was becoming restive. Bishop

---

50   The examination by the commissioners was known as the quest, or in modern terms, inquest. The historical term "quest" is used here throughout.
51   Wriothesley C. A. *Chronicle of England*, Camden Society, Second Series, 1875, XI, pp. 155–56.
52   Strype J. *Ecclesiastical Memorials of the Church of England*, 1823, I, pt. i, p. 598.

Bonner of London lamented in May 1546 that "there are more heretics now than in the last three or four years". Reporting to the Council that several people in Essex had been found guilty of "offences against the Blessed Sacrament of the Altar", he was yet very nervous about how to proceed. He had instructed the sheriff to "spare them execution until the King's pleasure is further known" and he begged the royal pardon, "if we have done, committed or neglected anything appertaining to our duties".[53] The enemies of reform were experiencing growing frustration and the acquittal of Anne and her associates rubbed salt into their wounds. It was insufferable to the guardians of Catholic truth that a shameless countrywoman could cock a snook at them because she had friends in high places, but as long as the king persisted in rejecting a wholesale purge their hands were tied.

At this point we must leave Anne's story and see how major events were playing out at the centre of power. The events of 1545–46 have a distinct air of déjà vu. Three decades earlier, Henry VIII had gone off to war in France in league with Europe's leading Catholic champion, Ferdinand II of Aragon. Now he crossed the Channel to confront the French in alliance with the Emperor Charles V. As before, he enjoyed some minor military triumphs. As before, he was abandoned by his comrade-in-arms, who made a separate peace with the enemy. As before, the adventure proved as expensive as it was pointless. And, as before, the person chosen to keep the home fires burning in the king's absence was his queen regent.

Catherine attended scrupulously to her duties. She supervised the raising of levies in order to send military reserves to the front line. She despatched cash and materiel to Henry. She interviewed diplomats and received reports from royal officials in the North who were keeping an eye on Scotland. When a Scottish ship was captured by chance and turned out to be carrying French envoys, it was Catherine who perused the seized messages and decided what was important enough to be sent on to her husband. She maintained

---

53   *L & P*, XX, pt. iii, 836.

a steady correspondence with Henry that was businesslike, affectionate – and devout. The interception of the Franco-Scottish correspondence was, she assured the king, "ordained, I doubt not, of God, to the intent your Highness might thereby certainly understand the crafty dealings and jugglings of [the Scots]".[54] To the modern eye, this and similar assurances of divine approval read like sycophancy but, as we have seen, all Henry VIII's policy was predicated on the conviction that he stood in a special relationship with God. Catherine shared this belief.

It is from around this time that we have the first concrete evidence about Catherine Parr's faith. We know the names of those she chose as friends and advisers. More importantly, we have her own writings. The queen wrote three devotional works between 1544 and 1547. It was not unknown for English ladies of high social station to commit to writing their own pious reflections. What was, up to this time, unique was for them to publish such works under their own name. Women were expected to defer to their menfolk in matters of religion and certainly not to air their views for general readership. But the times they were a-changing and, particularly, Renaissance influences from the Continent were impacting on life in royal courts.

As high-born ladies began to enjoy the educational opportunities of their menfolk they shared their ideas and beliefs via the intellectual network and in their own households. The salon presided over by a wealthy and cultured lady who surrounded herself with poets, musicians and scholars, and delighted to indulge in debate on all the latest in-vogue ideas and beliefs, made its appearance, first in Italy and then in lands north of the Alps. And some members of the female intelligentsia began venturing into print. The most celebrated such "bluestocking" in northern Europe was Margaret of Angoulême (1492–1549), known, after her marriage to Henry II of Navarre (1525), as Margaret of Navarre. This remarkable lady, beloved sister and confidante of Francis I of France, enjoyed fame far and wide as an avant-garde cultural and spiritual influence. Among the members of

---

54 *L&P*, XIX, pt. i, 1019.

her humanist circle was Jacques Lefèvre d'Étaples, translator of the Bible into French, Clément Marot, who was forced to flee to Strasbourg for lampooning the theological establishment and the famous satirist François Rabelais. Margaret herself produced a volume of picaresque tales, making fun of the clergy. But in more serious vein she translated one of Luther's books and composed a personal verse testimony of 1,400 lines – *Miroir de L'âme Pécheresse* (*Mirror of the Sinful Soul*) – which owed a great deal to the doctrine of salvation by faith alone. As Queen of Navarre, Margaret provided a haven to people of many persuasions who were fleeing persecution.

As we seek to understand the religious life of Europe in the middle year of the sixteenth century, it is less than helpful to put labels such as "Catholic" and "Protestant" on many of the active thinkers of the age. In the bustling marketplace of competing ideas, eager and troubled souls were working out their salvation with fear and trembling (Philippians 2:12). A slight digression might be valuable to set Catherine and her entourage in a wider perspective.

In 1538 the charismatic preacher Bernardino Ochino was general of the Italian Capuchin order of ascetic and scholarly friars. He was moving towards a Lutheran position on grace and faith and making a considerable impact on the crowds who came to hear him. There were several influential women among them who supported the itinerant preacher and defended him from the ecclesiastical authorities. Ochino belonged to the radical fringe within Catholicism known as the *Spirituali* because of an emphasis on the ongoing work of the Holy Spirit in the life of the believer. Such teaching with its roots in Christian mysticism was not unorthodox. Several senior clergy were members of the movement, as was the leading humanist philosopher and biblical scholar Juan Valdes (d.1541). What was troubling to the Vatican was the *Spirituali's* stress on the Bible as the sole authority and the fact that Ochino and his friends engaged in dialogue with Luther, Calvin, and other Reformation leaders. Naples was the spiritual nursery of this exotic plant where it was nurtured by the wealthy and well-connected Giulia Gonzaga. From there it was transplanted to other centres.

Ochino's spiritual pilgrimage was not over. His reflections on Scripture took him further and further away from the official teachings of the church. On his travels throughout northern Italy he was often welcomed to the salons of pious noble ladies who protected him from the mounting hostility of the Inquisition. It was thanks to the help of Vittoria Colonna, Marchioness of Pescara, that he eventually made his escape to Calvin's Geneva in 1542. Vittoria was the most famous female writer of her day, celebrated among the intelligentsia for her poetry, devotional works and letters. Ochino's fame went before him and, soon after Henry VIII's death, Archbishop Cranmer invited him to England.

The salon as a place for discussing the latest cultural and religious ideas did not become established in England until the reign of Elizabeth I but Queen Catherine would certainly have known about the initiatives being taken by educated women abroad. She certainly took seriously her role as spiritual guide to her own household. During Henry's absence on campaign, Cranmer was charged to pay regular visits to the regent and it is inconceivable that they did not discuss the latest personalities and events in the religious life of Europe. Both of them were working out their own salvation and considering their responses to the burning theological issues of the day.

Catherine had a largely free hand in selecting the members of her inner circle but that does not mean that they were all evangelically inclined. There were some ladies who would reasonably have expected to be among the queen's closest attendants. Wives of royal councillors were among this number. Thus, as well as known reformers, such as Lady Suffolk, Lady Hertford, and Lady Lisle, conservative sympathisers including Lady Wriothesley, wife of the Lord Chancellor, were also members of the queen's chamber. Not only was Jane Wriothesley one of the leaders of the reactionary group on the Council, she was the niece of another. Her uncle was Stephen Gardiner and her half-brother was Germain Gardiner, who had recently been executed for his part in the plot against Cranmer. A rather strange letter from Catherine to Jane has survived which suggests that the relationship between the two ladies was not of the warmest. Jane's young son died in the summer of 1544 and the queen wrote to express her condolence:

Good my lady Wriothesley,

Understanding it hath pleased God, of late, to disinherit
your son of this world, of intent he should become
partner and chosen heir of the everlasting inheritance
(which calling and happy vocation ye may rejoice), yet
when I consider you are a mother by flesh and nature,
doubting how you can give place quietly to the same,
inasmuch as Christ's mother, endued with all godly virtues,
did utter a sorrowful, natural passion of her Son's death,
whereby we have all obtained everlastingly to live: therefore
… I have thought with mine own hand to recommend
unto you my simple counsel and advice, desiring you not
to so utter your natural affection by inordinate sorrow that
God have cause to take you as a m[urm]urer against His
appointments and ordinances.

For what is excessive sorrow but a plain evidence against
you, that your inward mind doth repine against God's
doings, and a declaration that you are not contented that
God hath put your son – by nature, but His by adoption – in
possession of the heavenly kingdom? Such as have doubted
of the everlasting life to come doth sorrow and bewail the
departure hence. But those which be persuaded that, to die
here, is life again, do rather hunger for death, and count
it a foolish thing to bewail it as an utter destruction. How
much, Madam, are you to be counted godly wise that will
and can prevent, through your godly wisdom, knowledge,
and humble submission, that thing that time would at
length finish? If you lament your son's death, you do him
great wrong and show yourself to sorrow for the happiest
thing there ever came to him, being in the hands of his best
Father. If you be sorry for your own commodity, you show
yourself to live to yourself …[55]

---

55   Mueller J. (ed.) *Katherine Parr – Complete Works and Correspondence*,
Chicago, 2011, pp. 80–81.

Such chiding must have been difficult to take, particularly from a woman who had never had children of her own. Catherine, it seems, could not resist the opportunity to deliver a homily on divine grace and correct what she regarded as an inappropriate reluctance to submit to the will of God.

It was about the same time that Catherine published her first book. It is intriguing for several reasons. *Psalms or Prayers taken out of Holy scripture* was produced by the king's printer, Thomas Berthelet. Although the editor is not named there is enough circumstantial evidence for a clear attribution to the queen. One extant copy was a gift from Catherine to her husband on the eve of his departure for France and the book includes a Prayer for the King, which was Catherine's own composition. The other pages are devoted to translations into English of a collection of Latin prayers published some twenty years earlier by a writer whose name is also suppressed in the queen's book. And for a very good reason. The original was the work of Bishop John Fisher, executed in 1535 for refusing to acknowledge Henry as head of the English church and subsequently revered among Catholics as a martyr. Catherine could not associate herself with Fisher's treason but she did value his spiritual insights. Catherine's first venture into publication, thus, cautions us about being free with sectarian labels.

It also provides a valuable window into the queen's devotional life. The book, which had a small print run and was probably intended to be used as a royal gift to friends and household members, was probably suggested by George Day, Bishop of Chichester. Day had been Fisher's chaplain and, though not a defender of the papalist position, was conservative in matters of theology. Catherine appointed him as her almoner and he may have assisted her in the work of translation. Unsurprisingly, the queen nowhere departed from Catholic orthodoxy in this text. For example, she retained "doing penance" as the rendering of *poenitentia*, rather than the reformers' preferred reading, "repentance". But she was clearly familiar with Tyndale's version of Scripture and used his wording in less contentious areas.

The writer brought together hundreds of Bible passages and, with intense passion, interposed the sinfulness of men and the unmerited grace of God:

Of a truth there is no mortal man which hath not done wickedly; nor there is any righteous on earth, which doeth good and sinneth not.

Yet because mercy is in Thy hand, O Lord although Thou be dreadful, my hope is in Thee, in whom my soul trusteth.

My soul looketh for Thee, because mercy and plentiful redemption is with Thee.

Her graphic description of Christ's physical suffering is reminiscent of Grünewald's Isenheim altarpiece in its shocking ultra realism:

Behold Thine own sweet Son, how all His body was drawn and stretched forth on the cross.

Look upon all the parts of His body, from the crown of the head unto the sole of the foot; and no pain shall be found like unto His pain.

Behold, O loving father, the blessed head of Thy dear Son, crowned with sharp thorns, and the blood running down upon His godly visage.

Behold His tender body, how it is scourged. His naked breast is stricken and beaten; His bloody side is thrasted through. His heart panteth; His sinews be stretched forth. His goodly eyes dazzle and lose their sight; His princely face is wan and pale. His pleasant tongue is inflamed for pain; His inward parts wax dry and stark. His arms both, blue and wan, be stiff. His bones be plucked one from another. His beautiful legs be feeble and weak; and the streams of blood issuing out of His body run down apace upon His feet.[56]

---

56   Mueller 2011, pp. 239, 235.

This work of emotional, interiorized devotion was not Catherine's only contribution to raising the spiritual temperature in England. She was determined to use her newfound authority to encourage people to study the Bible in the vernacular. This would demand a publishing programme aimed at a far wider readership than that of the *Psalms and Prayers*. To this end she energetically sponsored the translation of Erasmus's *Paraphrases*. These were Latin commentaries on all the New Testament books except Revelation and were written between 1517 and 1524. These laymen's guides to the Bible were welcomed in reform circles but regarded with some suspicion by Catholic authorities (the Council of Trent placed an Italian version on the Index of Banned Books). There was nothing overtly heretical about Erasmus's work, but it went to the very heart of the Reformation conflict: should ordinary people be encouraged to read the Bible for themselves? The Lateran Council as long ago as 1215 had vetoed the very idea on the grounds that "such is the depth of divine Scripture that, not only the simple and illiterate, but even the prudent and learned are not fully sufficient to try to understand it".[57] Cromwell and his band of scholars had laboured long to bring into being the Great Bible and to persuade Henry VIII to sanction it. The king, as we have seen, had backtracked on this decision but the Act for the Advancement of True Religion had been a prime example of shutting the stable door after the horse had bolted. There were now only two ways forward: to withdraw all English Bibles and stiffen the penalties against the peddlers of Scripture or to distribute scholarly texts to help people understand the word of God correctly. The first option was no longer realistic. Therefore, evangelicals, humanists and not a few Catholics saw translating of the *Paraphrases* as the best way forward. Queen Catherine became the figurehead of this movement.

She commissioned several scholars to undertake Erasmus's individual commentaries and appointed the Latinist and pedagogue and writer of sophisticated court comedies Nicholas Udall to collate

---

57   See Lambert M. *Medieval Heresy – Popular Movements from the Gregorian Reform to the Reformation*, Oxford, 1992, p. 73.

the various contributions. Udall was one of the first self-declared Lutherans, however, and as his later career during the reign of Mary Tudor demonstrates, he did not allow religious conviction to stand in the way of advancement. It is quite likely that the *Paraphrases* project brought the scholar and the future queen together, for Princess Mary was one of Catherine Parr's chosen translators and began work on John's gospel (but was obliged by illness to abandon the task). For all the zealous energy that went into this book, it had to wait until after Henry's death before it could appear in print – evidence of just how cautious advocates of reform were in the last months of the old king's reign. Undoubtedly, evangelicals made the running in the *Paraphrases* endeavour. One of the translators, Oxford scholar Thomas Caius, expressed clearly in a letter to Catherine the faith he knew they both shared:

> Who so knoweth Christ aright surely believeth to attain salvation by Him only, who sayeth: Come unto me, all ye that do travail and are charged, and I shall refresh you. The very office of Christ is to save, and therefore He was called, by the high wisdom of God, "Jesu", that is as much to say as "a Saviour", because (so saith the angel in Matthew) "He shall save the people from their sins." So that it appeareth hereby how greatly they are deceived that think to be saved by any other mean than by Christ, or that make themselves quarter-saviours with Him, ascribing any part of their salvation unto their own works and deservings.[58]

But the queen could not show herself to be openly partisan or advance beyond the doctrinal position held by her husband. Extending the use of the vernacular in the devotional and liturgical life of English Christians was a cautious way of eroding the dominance of the traditionalist priesthood. Cranmer – as Catherine certainly knew – was working steadily towards the introduction of an English prayer book.

---

58   Mueller 2011, p. 109.

Catherine's pen was not inactive in these months. In November 1545 a new book came from the press of the king's printer: *Prayers or Meditations, wherein the mind is stirred patiently to suffer all afflictions here, to set at naught the vain prosperity of this world and always to long for the everlasting felicity: Collected out of holy works by the most virtuous and gracious Princess Catherine, queen of England, France and Ireland.* Now there was no cover of anonymity: this little devotional tract became the earliest English text published by a woman in her own name. It must have had the blessing of the king and was an immediate hit with his people, running to thirteen editions by the end of the century. *Prayers or Meditations* was a "bridge" project. It was based upon the extremely popular *Imitation of Christ* by Thomas à Kempis, but shortened the medieval original and "de-Catholicized" it. The stress is not on those spiritual exercises that could elevate the soul to the heavenlies but on the grace of God, working sanctification in the heart of the believer:

> O Lord Jesu, make that possible by grace, that is to me impossible by nature ... Remember Thy mercies, and fill my heart with plenty of Thy grace: for Thou would not that Thy works in me should be made in vain.[59]

Catherine's writings were designed to influence a wide readership but there were three individuals on whom she was particularly desirous to make an impression. Even before her marriage to Henry she had taken a close interest in his children, Mary (aged 27), Elizabeth (10), and Edward (7). Catherine and Mary had been friends in the household of Catherine of Aragon, but the two princesses had been *personae non gratae* at court since their bastardization and young Edward, as heir to the throne, spent most of his time in the country to reduce the possibility of contagion. Catherine worked hard to bring the king and his children together, and under her gentle persuasion Henry, during his last two-and-a-half years, enjoyed an experience of family life such as he had never known. When he went off to war the queen

---

59   Mueller 2011, pp. 399, 417.

brought her step-children together at Hampton Court. There and during the subsequent progress through other royal mansions they bonded and Catherine's charges developed a real affection for her as she was the closest thing to a mother that they knew. The queen kept a close eye on the education of the two younger children and was in frequent contact with the humanist scholars who tutored them. Elizabeth, especially, was a gifted child. Her talents, her moderate evangelical leanings and her affection for her step-mother are indicated in the New Year's gifts she presented to Catherine and Henry. In 1545 the queen received an English translation of Margaret of Navarre's *Mirror of the Sinful Soul.* The following year Elizabeth's present to her father was Catherine's *Prayers or Meditations*, carefully translated by the princess into Latin, French, and Italian.

CHAPTER 8

The Year of Crisis

 B oth the chronology and the psychology of the events of 1546 have always been the subject of much debate among historians. What all are agreed on is that conflict between religious conservatives and reformers grew increasingly tense as it became evident that the reign of the great dictator was nearing its end. Having enjoyed his last great adventure, defying nature by riding to war with younger, healthier captains, Henry returned to conclude by diplomacy what had been started by military conflict and to settle the religious differences in his own kingdom. The two were bound up together. As ever, they involved playing off the Spanish emperor and the king of France against each other, with the pope always hovering in the background determined to regain his foothold in England. Internal religious discord was an embarrassment to Henry and it was soon after his return that he made his impassioned plea for unity to Parliament; but, inevitably, Catholic and evangelical activists interpreted this appeal differently, using it to expose the "errors" of their rivals, rather than curbing the excesses of their friends.

The radical, John Hooper, writing from his haven in Strasbourg, passed on a very gloomy analysis of the situation in England to his friend Henry Bullinger in Zurich:

> The impious mass, the most shameful celibacy of the clergy, the invocation of saints, auricular confession, superstitious abstinence from meats, and purgatory, were never before held by the people in greater esteem than at the present moment ...

The chief supporters of the gospel in England are dying every hour: many very illustrious personages have departed within these two years; the lord chancellor Audley, the duke of Suffolk, [Sir Edward] Baynton, the queen's first lord of the bedchamber; Poinings, the king's deputy at Boulogne; Sir Thomas Wyatt, known throughout the whole world for his noble qualities, and a most zealous defender of yours and Christ's religion; Dr Butts, a physician who had the charge of the king's person; all these were of the privy council, and real favourers of the gospel, and promoted the glory of God to the utmost of their power. They all died of the plague and fever; so that the country is now left altogether to the bishops, and those who despise God and all true religion.[60]

But the reformist cause was far from silenced. Dr Edward Crome, the vicar of St Mary Aldermary, who had been examined back in 1539–40 and forced to recant, was once more preaching against purgatory and masses for the dead.[61] And once more he was obliged to make a public disavowal of his "heresies" at Easter in 1546.

Crome had a considerable following in London but he was very far from being the only unorthodox preacher in the city. Several people were called before the Council, or the Lord Mayor, or the bishop, accused of delivering or listening to unorthodox sermons, discussing such sermons and circulating "lewd books and writings among light persons, which medille further in these matters than their capacities be able to comprehend".[62] There were even strolling players performing satirical interludes making fun of the clergy and their teaching. The authorities were at their wits' end to know how to deal with this escalating problem. Burnings and imprisonments had proved counterproductive and the king had shown himself averse to prolonged persecution.

60　Robinson H. (ed.) *Original Letters Relative to the English Reformation*, Cambridge, 1846, pp. 36–37.

61　See p. 59.

62　Brigden S. *London and the Reformation*, Oxford, 1989, p. 365.

Trial and error suggested that the best way to bring this plague under control was to locate the most influential heretics and remove their sting by forcing them to make public recantations. But the heresy hunters on the Council were not at all clear how far or how fast they should proceed. Their fingers had been burned more than once. Therefore, they asked the king what they should do, particularly with persons of "quality", being loath "to offend in doing too much, or too little". It is against this nervous background of delicately balanced forces that the last acts of Anne Askew's story were played out.[63]

She had not been keeping a low profile since her brush with the quest and was well known to the authorities as a frequenter of radical sermons, a member of covert Bible-study groups, and a woman of breeding with influential friends at court. She was not someone who could be pulled in off the street and bullied into recantation. The impression we gain of her from her own writing is of an intelligent woman with a prodigious knowledge of the Bible. During her interrogation she quoted by heart texts she had learned from no less than nineteen books of Scripture. This, in itself, was an irritant to her examiners. To be lectured on the word of God by a mere woman was intolerable for them. She was brave, bold or, as her enemies would describe her, brazen. When the heat was on, prominent evangelicals such as Dr Crome and Nicholas Shaxton (former Bishop of Salisbury) wilted and publicly rejected their former "errors". Anne was given many opportunities to follow suit and was urged to do so by enemies, friends, and even by prominent councillors, but she held stubbornly to her belief. She could not be argued or threatened out of her convictions and, since arguments and threats were the only weapons her enemies had, they were forced into the position of losing face or committing her to suffer the ultimate fate of heretics.

The fact that Anne was ready – even eager – to push her accusers to embrace the ultimate solution might suggest that she had a death wish. This was a common trait of Anabaptists who saw in persecution and martyrdom the proof that they were

---

63   Brigden 1989, p. 366.

among the elect. One such, Anna Jansz of Rotterdam, left this typical testimony when she went to her death in 1539:

> I go the way which Christ Jesus, the eternal Word of
> the Father, the Shepherd of the sheep, who is the Life,
> Himself went ... Having passed through, He calls His
> sheep, and His sheep hear His voice and follow Him
> withersoever He goes; for this is the way to the true
> fountain (John 10:27; 4:14). This way was travelled by the
> royal priests, who came from the rising of the sun, as we
> read in Revelation, and entered into the ages of eternity ...
> White robes were given to them, and it was said to them:

> "Wait yet for a little season until the number of your
> brethren that are yet to be killed for the testimony of Jesus
> be fulfilled" (Revelation 6:9–11).[64]

There is no trace of such apocalypticism in Anne Askew's testimony. She did not set out to embrace martyrdom and when it drew near she sent an appeal to the king for clemency. Doubtless, many of her accusers regarded all radicals as tarred with the same brush; they were pestilential enemies of good order and potential disturbers of the king's peace. But within the "left wing" of the Reformation there were several nuances of belief. Before we chronicle Anne's last few months, can we therefore discover exactly what she did believe and how she might have come by her particular brand of evangelical theology?

By the mid-1540s the Lutheran corpus of belief (itemized in the Augsburg Confession of 1530) was regarded by many thinking evangelicals as merely a half-way house on the road to true doctrine. Many English scholars were travelling to Geneva, where Calvin held sway, Zurich, under the pastoral leadership of Henry Bullinger, and Strasbourg where the reformation of the church was led by Martin Bucer. In one or other of such cities

---

64   Krahn C. *Dutch Anabaptism: Origin, Spread, Life and Thought (1450–1600)*, The Hague, 1968, pp. 200–1.

English travellers found, or believed they had found, a perfect pattern of "Christian commonwealth", where church and state authorities worked in harmony in the service of the Gospel. The pastors and preachers in various reformed communities projected doctrinal "packages" which varied in some points, one from another. These differences of emphasis were of no great significance. Except one: as we have seen, the manner of Christ's presence in the mass, or eucharist, or Lord's Supper was an issue over which evangelical theologians contended fiercely and even bitterly. They all turned their back on the "priestly miracle" by which the celebrant claimed to effect real change in the elements of bread and wine but interpreted differently Christ's words, "This is my body ... this is my blood". Luther insisted on a literal understanding of the dominical statement, while the Swiss reformers favoured some kind of symbolic interpretation.

The first generation of English reformed theologians took their lead from Wittenberg, but as more and more books, pamphlets, and letters circulated between English evangelicals and their Continental counterparts, there was a decided shift of belief. An English ex-friar, Bartholomew Traheron, well captured this tentative change of emphasis when writing to his friend Bullinger:

> You must know that all our countrymen, who are
> sincerely favourable to the restoration of truth, entertain
> in all respects like opinions with you; and not only such
> as are placed at the summit of honour, but those who
> are ranked in the number of men of learning. I except
> the archbishop of Canterbury and Latimer, and a very
> few learned men besides; for from among the nobility I
> know not one whose opinions are otherwise than what
> they ought to be. As to Canterbury, he conducts himself
> in such a way, I know not how, as that the people do
> not think much of him, and the nobility regard him
> as lukewarm. In other respects he is a kind and good-
> natured man. As to Latimer, though he does not clearly
> understand the true doctrine of the eucharist, he is
> nevertheless more favourable than either Luther or even

Bucer. I am quite sure that he will never be a hindrance
to this cause. For, being a man of admirable talent, he
sees more clearly into the subject than the others, and
is desirous to come into our sentiments, but is slow
to decide, and cannot without much difficulty and
even timidity renounces an opinion which he has once
imbibed. But there is good hope that he will some time
or other come over to our side altogether. For he is so
far from avoiding any of our friends, that he rather seeks
their company, and most anxiously listens to them while
discoursing upon this subject, as one who is beyond
measure desirous that the whole truth may be laid open
to him, and even that he may be thoroughly convinced.[65]

The hesitation of Cranmer, Latimer, and other church leaders is
easily explained. As long as Henry VIII lived, England adhered
officially to the Catholic doctrine of the mass. In most heresy
trials the litmus test applied by the authorities was, "What do you
believe about Christ's presence in the sacrament of the altar?" Any
havering over the reply or direct rebuttal of transubstantiation was
enough to bring the examinee close to the stake. Traheron's letter
was written in August 1548 and, if his analysis is correct, some
of England's leading theologians were still only edging cautiously
towards the Zurich (that is, Zwinglian) doctrine of the Lord's
Supper which many prominent laymen were openly professing in
the freedom of a new reign. The essence of the Zwinglian position
was that bread and wine were "signs", representing but separate
from the things signified. The communion was not a re-enactment
of Calvary. The priest at the altar did not "make" Christ present
in his hands. God did not impart his grace *through* the elements.
Rather they reaffirmed that the worshipper had already received
grace. While receiving bread and wine in the mouth the believer
also fed on Christ in the heart by faith. By the time the first English
Prayer Book appeared in 1549 this had become the official doctrine
of the English church.

---

65   Robinson 1846, p. 320.

As we have seen, this was the understanding of Anne's friend and fellow believer, the courtier from Nottinghamshire, John Lascelles, who wrote:

> I do steadfastly believe, that where the bread is broken according to the ordinance of Christ, the blessed and immaculate Lamb is present to the eyes of our faith, and so we eat his flesh and drink his blood, which is to dwell with God and God with us.[66]

Was Anne, then, like John, an adherent of that Swiss-born faith that was to become the new English orthodoxy? Or had she, somewhere along the line, picked up a more extreme, "Anabaptist" theology? This is how she summed up her view of the eucharist:

> My belief which I wrote to the Council was this. That the Sacramental bread was left us to be received with thanksgiving, in remembrance of Christ's death, the only remedy of our souls to recover. And that thereby we also receive the whole benefits and fruits of his most glorious passion. Then would they needs know whether the bread in the box were God or no. I said: God is a spirit, and will be worshipped in spirit and truth. John 4 Then they demanded. Will you plainly deny Christ to be in the Sacrament? I answered that I believe faithfully the eternal Son of God not to dwell there.

She went further:

> The same Son of God, that was born of the Virgin Mary, is now glorious in heaven, and will come again from thence at the latter day like as he went up – Acts i. And as for that ye call your God, it is a piece of bread: for a more proof

---

66 Foxe J. *Acts and Monuments*, Volume V, p. 552.

thereof … let it lie in the box but iii months, and it will be mouldy, and so turn to nothing that is good. Whereupon I am persuaded, that it can not be God. [67]

This suggests memorialism, the kind of assertion of the "divine absence", made by several Anabaptists. It was also a mark of Zwingli's early followers, but was later abandoned in favour of a more sophisticated understanding of God's activity in the sacrament. There was certainly nothing intellectually sophisticated about Anne's religion. And, perhaps, therein lies the answer to our question. Doctrinal consensus among the members of London's evangelical underworld was lacking. Certainly, there was a strong framework consisting of the primacy of Scripture, rejection of "priestcraft" and "papist" ceremonial, justification of the individual by faith, and motivation of the individual by the indwelling Holy Spirit. But on the finer details of theology such as the nature of the church, attitude towards religious images, and precise definition of the sacraments there were various ideas sloshing around. Therefore, it is probably a mistake to try to locate Anne firmly within any one radical tradition. What we can say without hesitation, having read her own accounts of her trials, is that she was an ardent Bible student whose convictions were derived, first and foremost, from daily study of the holy text. We must, therefore, consider her two unique documents.

In March 1546, Anne came once more to the attention of the authorities. The reason seems to have been that she had become such a celebrity in the evangelical world that a widely broadcasted recantation would have been a valuable publicity coup for the enemies of religious radicalism. On 10 March, Anne was conveyed to Saddlers' Hall, on the north side of West Cheap, a stone's throw from St Paul's Cathedral, there to be examined again by the Six Articles commissioners. [68] It is not clear whether this quest was held

---

67   Beilin E. V. (ed.) *The Examinations of Anne Askew*, Oxford, 1996, p. 184.

68   Some earlier writers ascribe this arrest to March 1545, thus making it the first occasion on which Anne ran foul of the authorities. In this they were following the accounts of Bale and Foxe who gave the date as 10

in public. The chairman in such proceedings seems to have enjoyed the freedom to admit observers or proceed *in camera*. Christopher Dare, the member of the Common Council designated to conduct Anne's examination, may well have wished to keep the general public at bay in what was a high-profile case. It certainly seems that none of the accused's influential friends were present. Anne was on her own.

Thanks to Anne's own account, published later, we can see how this secular tribunal went about its work. They clearly had a set of stock questions to ask and were not very adept at understanding the religious issues underlying them. Dare first tried to draw Anne out on her doctrine of the eucharist: was the consecrated bread *really* the body of Christ?[69] The prisoner declined to answer with a straight "No", which would, undoubtedly, have resulted in her being immediately handed over to the ecclesiastical authorities. Dare countered by stating that the quest was in possession of a sworn testimony from a witness who accused Anne of scorning the sacrament by saying "God dwelleth not in temples made with hands". This turned out to be something of an own goal; Anne riposted with quotations from the book of Acts (7:56; 17:24) to confirm that Christ dwells in heaven and not corporally on earth. She had now gained the upper hand in the exchange and when Dare lamely asked how she interpreted and applied Bible texts, Anne replied with mockery: "I will not cast my pearls before swine: acorns be good enough."

Dare now reverted to his list of questions and asked her opinions on the priesthood and auricular confession. In each case

---

March 1545. But the sixteenth-century accounts used the old calendar employed in legal and official circles whereby the new year was not begun until 26 March. There can be no doubt that the correct date is 10 March 1546, as was pointed out by Pratt in his edition of *Acts and Monuments*, V, p. 836. Only this dating makes sense of the sequence of Anne's three trials. Furthermore the accounts specifically name the Lord Mayor who examined her as Sir Martin Bowes and he was not installed until November 1545.

69   A full account of Anne's two 1546 trials can be found in Beilin 1996, pp. 19ff.

the young lady referred her hearers to the relevant portions of Scripture without committing herself in any way. The examiner now moved on to more dangerous matters.

DARE: What do you think of the King's Book?

ANNE: I have never read it.

Dare's next question was suggested by the knowledge that Anabaptists claimed to be beyond the reach of human laws because their only guide was the prompting of the Holy Spirit within.

DARE: Do you have the Spirit of God within you?

ANNE: If I do not, I am but a reprobate or a castaway.

The chairman now called in the theological light cavalry in the form of a learned priest. This failed because the wary interviewee declined to be led into the deep waters of sacramental doctrine. Her own later comment on the priest's attempted interrogation was: "None other answer would I make him, because I perceived him a papist." After a couple more, equally frustrating attempts to get Anne to declare unequivocally that she rejected the statutory definition of Christian doctrine, Dare was at a loss. Had the examinee been a semi-literate serving wench he would have known how to deal with her but this haughty, well-connected gentlewoman presented a real problem. He could release her or send her for trial by a church court. Either might have got him into trouble. Dare decided to duck the responsibility. He sent Anne, under escort, to higher authority – the Lord Mayor, Sir Martin Bowes.

Bowes (c.1497–1560) was a stout pillar of the mercantile establishment. He served five terms as Prime Warden of the Goldsmiths' Company, had been an alderman since 1536 and was currently Under-Treasurer of the Tower Mint. Nothing is known of his religious sympathies during the crisis years of the early Reformation but it is reasonable to assume that he did not allow them to hinder his material prospects. By the time he made his will in Elizabeth's reign he was ardently Protestant, leaving charitable bequests and money for the preaching of sermons. Whether he had developed strong convictions or simply moved with the times we cannot tell but it is reasonable to think that his involvement in Anne Askew's persecution must have left its mark on him.[70]

Bowes took the precaution of involving a leading cleric in his interrogation of this impertinent young lady. Dr John Standish was the bishop's chancellor. His own position on Bible-quoting troublemakers had been made quite clear in a book published in 1544 in which he had "proved" from ancient authors that the word of God should not be translated into the vernacular. It was Standish who took the lead in this stage of the investigation although Bowes did raise a point that is quite revealing about public perceptions

---

70 There is some contradiction among the authorities as to what happened next. Anne's own account published by Bale states clearly "then they had me from thence to my Lord Mayor". Archdeacon Loud, a scholar and tutor in the pay of the upwardly mobile Sir Richard Rich, who was in 1546, Solicitor General and Sir Richard Southwell (a member of the Privy Council), expanded on this in a letter to Foxe with the express intention of providing the martyrologist with more information. Yet his narrative was written some fifteen troubled years after the events described and Foxe did not apparently think sufficiently highly of it to incorporate it in later editions of his *Book of Martyrs*. According to Loud, Anne was immediately lodged in the Tower, whither the Lord Mayor, Sir Martin Bowes, repaired to interview her. The improbability of her being lodged in the Tower by the quest hardly needs stressing and Loud is almost certainly confusing this period of Anne's persecution with a later one when she was imprisoned in the Tower (this was only after her conviction as an unrepentant heretic). Furthermore, Loud has some fun at Bowes's expense and seems intent upon ridiculing him by putting into his mouth some absurd questions which enabled Anne to ridicule him more effectively. Eventually, according to Loud, the assembly broke up with much laughter and the complete confusion of the Lord Mayor. We are probably wiser to trust in Anne's, simpler, account of this particular section of her examination.

of what evangelicals really did believe. Did Anne think, he asked, that if a crumb of the consecrated bread fell to the ground and was eaten by a mouse, that creature did actually ingest God? This old canard had been doing the rounds for a century or more and was commonly believed to be a standard Lollard objection to transubstantiation. Anne treated it with the disdain it deserved: "I made them no answer, but smiled."

Standish took a different tack, based on the very text by which she set so much store. St Paul, he pointed out, had expressly forbidden women to dabble with holy things. Anne was not to be caught out. The apostle's prohibition in 1 Corinthians 14, she explained, only applied to women teaching in the congregation. Had Standish, she asked, ever encountered a woman preaching from the pulpit? When he replied in the negative, she retorted that he should "find no fault in poor women, unless they had offended against the law".

Bowes now seems to have decided that a spell of solitary confinement might break Anne's stubborn will. He consigned her to the Lord Mayor's prison, the Compter (or Counter), in Bread Street, with the instruction that she was to be allowed no visitors apart from a maid to attend to her meals and other necessities. He had no desire to see her suffer the punishment designated for unrepentant heretics. What he wanted to obtain was a simple recantation which would allow her to go free and display the triumph of orthodox belief over error. Incarceration in this establishment might not have been very harsh, since prisoners could occupy quarters and enjoy comforts dependent on their ability to pay. However, the officers had a bad name for exploiting their charges and, within a decade, the Bread Street Compter was closed down.

In these drear conditions Anne was obliged to remain for twelve days. Hoping that the experience would encourage her to reconsider her position, the Bishop of London, Edmund Bonner, sent a priest to reason with her. This resulted in a tedious repetition of questions Anne had already been troubled with. Basically her new interlocutor was concerned to discover whether she was a dutiful daughter of holy Church. Would she make her confession?

Did she intend to receive the sacrament at Easter? Her response was that she would happily receive spiritual counsel from a priest she trusted (that is, one of her own persuasion) and that she certainly regarded Easter communion as important. The atmosphere of this interview was less abrasive than her earlier ordeals. Perhaps the anonymous cleric was impressed by Anne's sincerity. For whatever reason, he "departed thence with many fair words".

It was 23 March before she was allowed any personal visitors. Then her "Cousin Britain" was admitted to the Compter. All we know of him is that he was a law man probably at Gray's Inn.[71] He tried to arrange for the prisoner's release on bail. He approached the Lord Mayor, who directed him to Standish, who was not prepared to take any initiative without the sanction of the Bishop of London. It was at this point that Edmund Bonner took a direct interest in Anne's case.

"Bloody" Bonner was one of the main hate figures of the age, as recorded in Protestant literature. He was depicted as a persecutor who enjoyed beating his victims during private investigations and relished consigning "heretics" to the fires of Smithfield. This reputation was gained largely during the subsequent reign of Mary Tudor, but his determination to purge the realm of erroneous doctrine began in the 1540s when he issued his own index of banned books and attacked obstinate evangelicals with mounting vigour. He had good cause for such determination for his diocese was more infected than any other with the New Learning. In this case Bonner seems to have approached the business with fair-minded courtesy – at least initially. He offered to allow Anne the support of several of her friends. Accordingly, at three o'clock on 25 March Cousin Britain arrived with several others from the inns of court, including Edmund Butts, a younger son of Sir William, the king's late physician, and Edward Hall, the Tudor chronicler. Also present was one "Richard", a servant of Sir Anthony Denny, the member of the Privy Chamber closest to the king – clear

---

71   There were several families in Lincolnshire and East Anglia by the name of Britain though with several variant spellings but it has not, so far, been possible to connect the South Kelsey Askews with any of them.

evidence of the high-profile nature of this trial. The bishop came down to his great chamber with Dr Standish and other clergy. When all were seated, Anne Askew's next examination began.

Bonner started, benignly, urging her to speak anything that was on her mind:

BONNER: Now, if a man has a wound and goes to a surgeon with it he cannot receive treatment until the wound is uncovered. In just the same way, I cannot help you until I know what your conscience is burdened with.

ANNE: My Lord, my conscience is clear on all things. It might appear odd if a surgeon were to lay a plaster on healthy skin.

BONNER: Very well, then you force me to lay to your charge your own reported words, which are these: you said that he that doth receive the sacrament from the hands of an evil priest, or a sinner, receiveth the devil and not God.

ANNE: I never spoke any such words. What I said to the quest and to my Lord Mayor, and what I now say again, was that the wickedness of the priest cannot hurt me, but in spirit and in faith, I receive nonetheless the body and blood of Christ.

BONNER: What a saying is this! In spirit?

ANNE: My Lord, without faith and spirit I cannot receive him worthily.

BONNER: Did you say that after consecration the holy bread in the pyx is still only bread?

ANNE: No, my Lord. When I was asked that question I gave no answer.

BONNER: But you quoted certain passages of Scripture in order to refute the doctrine of the mass.

ANNE: I only quoted St Paul's words to the Athenians in Acts 17: "God liveth not in temples made with hands."

BONNER: Oh, and how do you interpret these words?

ANNE: I believe as the Scripture tells me, my Lord.

BONNER: Oh, then what if Scripture says the holy bread is the body of Christ?

ANNE: I believe as the Scripture teaches …

BONNER: Well and what, in your opinion, does the Scripture teach?

ANNE: Whatever Christ and his apostles taught, that I believe.

BONNER: And what did they teach about the sacrament of the altar?

To that direct question Anne made no reply. She was being very careful not to condemn herself. But to the bishop her silence seemed like prevarication. When he commented on her reticence she could not resist a pert reply: "Solomon says, 'a woman of few words is a gift of God'." The bishop persisted in his attempt to obtain a straight answer from her.

BONNER: Did you or did you not say that the mass is idolatry?

ANNE: No, my Lord. When the quest asked whether private masses relieved departed souls I answered: "What idolatry is this, that we should believe more in private masses, than in the healthsome death of the dear Son of God."

BONNER: What sort of an answer is that?

ANNE: A poor one, my Lord, but good enough for the question.

It was a case of irresistible force meeting immovable object. The interrogation went on for more than another hour, until shadows stretched themselves over the rushes on the floor and lights were called for. Bonner and Standish went over again all the questions that previous inquisitors had brought up, including Anne's behaviour in Lincoln. What particularly irked the bishop was Anne's knowledge of the Bible. "There are many people who read the Scriptures but fail to live by what they read," he said. Anne refused to be cowed but her reply must have struck the tribunal as somewhat arrogant:

My Lord, I would that all men knew of my conversation and living in all points; for I am so sure of myself at this hour that there are none able to prove any dishonesty by me. If you know any that can do it, I pray you bring them forth.

Bonner's patience was at an end. He went into another room and there had a statement written for her to sign. It read as follows:

Be it known to all faithful people, that as touching the blessed sacrament of the altar, I do firmly and undoubtedly believe, that after the words of consecration be spoken by the priest, according to the common usage of this Church of England, there is present really the body and blood of our Saviour, Jesus Christ, whether the minister which doth consecrate be a good man or a bad man … Also, whensoever the said sacrament is received, whether the receiver be a good man or a bad man, he doth receive it really and corporally. And, moreover I do believe that whether the said sacrament be then received of the minister or else reserved to be put into the pyx, or to be brought to any person that is impotent or sick, yet there is the very body and blood of our said Saviour. So that, whether the minister or the receiver be good or bad, yea whether the sacrament be received or reserved, always there is the blessed body of Christ really.

And this thing with all other things touching the sacrament and other sacraments of the church, and all things else touching the Christian belief, which are taught and declared in the King's Majesty's book, lately set forth for the erudition of the Christian people. I Anne Askew, otherwise called Anne Kyme, do truly and perfectly believe, and do here and now confess and acknowledge. And here I do promise that hence forth I shall never say or do anything against the premises, or against any of them. In witness whereof, I the said Anne have subscribed my name unto these presents.

Anne was called into the bishop's privy chamber. The document was read to her and she was asked to sign it. The crunch moment had arrived. Anne could submit or burn. Clearly everyone else in that room – friends and enemies – wanted to save her from the fire. Anne was left to struggle alone with her conscience.

She asked for a footnote to be added which stated that she believed as much of the confession "as the body of Scripture doth agree to". The bishop refused. He had had enough of equivocation. At last, she succumbed to pressure and added her name to the document. Now we come to a conflict in the evidence. In her account Anne insisted that she did add a clause to the final document: "I, Anne Askew do believe all manner of things contained in the faith of the Catholic Church." By this she meant the true, invisible body of Gospel believers, not the earthly institution. However, the document from which John Foxe quoted in the episcopal register contained no such subscription.[72] Foxe's explanation was that the confession was copied out again at a later date and the subscription omitted so that the authorities could claim that Anne had gone back on her oath. Against this it can be argued that Bonner is unlikely to have tolerated the addition which Anne (by her own report) made to the document, since it went a long way towards nullifying all that he was trying to achieve by making her sign a confession. Whatever the truth of the matter, the authorities were now possessed of a document which, whether tampered with or not, served to discredit Anne Askew in the eyes of her admirers and co-religionists.

Anne was returned to prison to await the final stage of her humiliating climbdown. The next day she was taken to the Guildhall where she had to listen while her confession was publicly read aloud. Only on the following day was Anne finally set at liberty. She wisely decided not to remain in London. The Court of Chancery had ordered her to return to her husband; the bishop had urged her to go back to her county; her friends persuaded her of the great danger she would be in if she remained in London. Probably Anne herself, emotionally exhausted by the events of the past fortnight and depressed by the thought that she had signed a confession and, in some degree, compromised her faith, only wanted to get away to spend some time in quiet with her Bible and her God. So, at the end of March, attended by her few servants, she took the road northwards.

And that should have been the end of the matter. It was not. Within weeks events took a sudden and sinister turn.

---

72   Foxe J. *Acts and Monuments*, Volume V, p. 543.

CHAPTER 9

Condemned by the Law

... forasmuch as I do well understand all kind of learning doth flourish amongst you in this age, as it did amongst the Greeks at Athens long ago, I require and desire you all not so to hunger for the exquisite knowledge of profane learning, that it may be thought the Greeks' university was but transposed or now in England again revived, forgetting our Christianity, since their excellency only did attain to moral and natural things. But, rather, I gently exhort you to study and apply those doctrines as means and apt degrees to the attaining, and setting forth the better Christ's reverent and most sacred doctrine, that ... Cambridge may be accounted rather an university of divine philosophy than of natural or moral, as Athens was.[73]

*I*n 1545 Parliament passed a Chantries Act, allowing for the confiscation of chantry lands and endowments – part of the strategy for financing Henry's French war. The authorities of Cambridge University, alarmed at the possible implications of this legislation for their own property, turned to Queen Catherine to ask for her intercession with her husband. She did raise the issue with Henry (though, in all likelihood, the universities were not under any threat) but, in her reply to the chancellor and vice-

---

73   Mueller J. (ed.) *Katherine Parr – Complete Works and Correspondence*, Chicago, 2011, pp. 115-16.

chancellor of 26 February 1546, she could not forbear to deliver a mini-sermon, in the words above.

We should not read too much about Catherine's core beliefs into this one letter but her reference to "divine philosophy" is certainly reminiscent of the "*philosophia Christi*", the intellectual defence of Bible-based faith advocated by Erasmus. It was thirty years since he had taught at Cambridge but his influence there was still strong. On an academic level there was much common ground between the Dutch scholar and Luther – rejection of medieval scholasticism, demand for church reform, insistence on the study of vernacular Scriptures as the basis for faith and morals and the necessity of an interiorized religion which was more important than external rituals. Where Erasmus and Luther parted company was over some of the finer points of doctrine (such as free will) and the German's belligerent rejection of those who disagreed with him. The two men had drunk from different streams. Luther had imbibed the brackish waters of *anfechtung*, an intense and unremitting spiritual conflict. Erasmus had quaffed from the limpid spring of reason. We can observe something of the same distinction between Catherine Parr and Anne Askew.

The gentlewoman's faith had been shaped by the tensions of her unhappy marriage and the abuse she had had to bear from her ecclesiastical opponents. These experiences had forced her back to the word of God, which she studied avidly in her search for divine guidance. The queen's spiritual journey, though no less sincere, had allowed her more leisure for reflection. As we have seen, Erasmus's *Paraphrases* played no small part in her spiritual pilgrimage. Within the confines of her own apartments she maintained a daily routine of devotional exercises and, as opportunity served, broached religious topics with her husband. She also kept up correspondence with her step-children. Genuine bonds of affection existed between the queen and Princess Elizabeth and Prince Edward. Catherine kept a close watch on the education of the royal children, even when the latter were lodged in rural palaces away from the court.

Several letters survive from Edward to his stepmother, who encouraged the correspondence partly to develop the boy's Latin style. The formal courtesies and conventional expressions of affection allow us little glimpse of the prince's real feelings, but in a letter of 12 May 1546 something of Edward's personality peeps out. In it the nine-year-old urges his step-mother to maintain a critical eye on his elder half-sister, some twenty years his senior:

> ... the only real love is the love of God. Preserve,
> therefore, I pray you, my dear sister Mary from all the wiles
> and enchantments of the evil one; and beseech her to
> attend no longer foreign dances and merriments which do
> not become a most Christian princess.[74]

That brief appeal speaks volumes – not only about the serious moralizing of this precocious boy, but also about the inclinations of the queen, for we can hardly imagine that Edward was expressing opinions with which he knew his step-mother would disagree. Both sender and recipient viewed temporal affairs and relationships *sub specie aeternitatis*, or in the light of eternity. Put more simply, it means that they tried to seek the will of God in everything, looking beyond or through their immediate circumstances to divine meanings, to ultimate realities. It was this extraterrestrial perspective that enabled believers like Anne Askew to face opprobrium and the prospect of painful death. Did it also embolden Catherine Parr to encourage her husband to set his mind on "things above", to deflect his attention from his physical pain and from the mental stresses of weighing the pros and cons of policy, to concentrate on doing only that which was pleasing to God? The answer to those questions must be "yes", for why else, she must have wondered, would God have raised her to her current position if not to help Henry make decisions for the benefit of his people, the good of his own soul, and the greater glory of God? Certainly, those among the royal advisers who did not share her religious convictions regarded her influence as a very real threat. It was the clash of rival convictions that led to high drama in the hectic summer of 1546.

It has become a commonplace to set the last months of Henry VIII's reign against the political background of faction fighting

---

74   Muller 2011, p. 116.

between "Catholic" and "Protestant" groups on the royal Council. This is deceptive, not because it is untrue, but because it is only half true. There *were* bitterly opposed parties on the advisory body of which the dominant members were Norfolk and Gardiner, for the conservative, pro-imperial clique, and Seymour and Dudley for those who were progressive in matters of religion and favoured rapprochement with France. However, these cannot be called "factions" if by the word we mean organized cabals with clearly defined policies and agreed strategies for implementing those policies. The post-1540 era was one characterized by governmental confusion. For three decades, the nation's affairs had been in the hands of a wilful dictator whose principles and whims had been translated into workable initiatives and, where necessary, modified by the obedient but pragmatic Wolsey and Cromwell. There had evolved an administrative partnership (admittedly unequal) between Crown, Council, and Parliament. In the years following the death of Cromwell two things happened: first, there was no longer a "first minister" directing the formulation and implementation of policy; and second, the gradual retreat of the king within his Privy Chamber forced by his disability placed his close personal servants at the centre of power, rather than his conciliar advisers. Add to this the fact that the groupings within the Council lacked cohesion and direction and what emerges is instability. Decisions were made on a day-to-day basis and depended on the king's mood and the displacement of the major personnel (that is, who was at court; who was away on diplomatic mission or war; who was absent by reason of illness; who was in disgrace). Personal contact had always been important with Henry who could be easily swayed by appeals to his generosity, good humour or vanity but now access was even more vital. Without knowledge of how the changeable king was disposed at any particular time, it was difficult to plan and execute consistent policy. We have seen how prosecutions under the Six Articles Act fluctuated over the years because officials were hesitant to appear too strict or too lenient. The same uncertainty also prevailed in other areas of government business. Thus the historian seeking to understand the changes and chances of the fleeting weeks and months of 1546 is obliged to peer through a shifting mist and try to make sense of events and personalities only partially and fleetingly observed.

In the summer of 1546, religious differences were not at the top of most people's agenda. What Henry's subjects wanted more than anything else was peace and stability. The imperial ambassador Chapuys was undoubtedly right when he observed about the conflict with France "every man of wit in England blasphemes at the war".[75] The people were overtaxed, had suffered the fear of possible invasion, and many had lost family members in the fighting. Those men who survived were scarcely better off than their fallen comrades.

> The soldiers coming from Calais and Boulogne were dying along the road from Dover to London and along the roads from London to every corner of the kingdom while trying to go to their homes. After they had come home, those who were well fell sick and those who were sick got worse and from this sickness and feebleness and pest they died in every part of England.[76]

Though the fighting had ceased, peace terms had not been agreed. The sticking point was Boulogne which had been captured by the English. Francis I was desperate for its return and Henry VIII was determined not to relinquish his only gain from the war. Until well into June, John Dudley, the Lord Admiral, and Edward Seymour, Earl of Hertford and commander of the land forces, were involved with their French counterparts at Calais, haggling over peace terms. When agreement was eventually reached, Seymour and Dudley had to make repeated trips across the Channel in connection with the ratification and implementation of the treaty terms. Gardiner, the most proactive of the conservative councillors, was also employed abroad as ambassador, but he returned from the imperial court in March and was, thereafter, present at most Council meetings.

---

75   L & P, XXI, pt. i, 984.

76   Davies M. B. (trans.) Extracts from the Welsh chronicle of Elis Gruffydd, in *Bulletin of the Faculty of Arts*, 11/1, Cairo, 1949, p. 94.

Gardiner's closest colleagues in the new wave of persecutions were Richard Rich and Thomas Wriothesley. The Lord Chancellor was, as we have seen, an avowed enemy of heretics. Richard Rich was a man particularly suited to lead a heresy hunt. Ambitious and unscrupulous, he had climbed over the broken careers of friends and patrons whom he had helped to ruin, in his ascent to high office. A colleague of Sir Thomas More at the Middle Temple, he had been the chief prosecution witness at More's trial. Favoured and elevated to the important and lucrative post of Chancellor of the Court of Augmentations by Thomas Cromwell, he actively participated in the Master Secretary's downfall. Employed in the 1530s as visitor of the doomed monasteries, he changed sides in 1540 and thereafter was a mainstay of Gardiner's faction.

But again we must be careful not to see the events of 1546 as a straightforward clash between two idealistically opposed political parties. All the major players were as much concerned with their own prospects as with their religious beliefs. This is well indicated by the doggedly conservative nobleman Thomas Howard, Duke of Norfolk. He held aloof from the summer's persecutions. Having reached the conclusion that the Seymours were unassailable, he swallowed his pride and tried to negotiate an alliance with the "upstart" family. The scheme, for which royal permission was obtained before the end of May, entailed the marriage of Thomas Seymour to Norfolk's daughter, the Duchess of Richmond, and the alliance of three of Norfolk's grandsons to three of Hertford's daughters.

This elaborate scheme was scuppered by the duke's own son, the Earl of Surrey, who was even more arrogant than his father and refused to debase himself by alliance with the Seymours. He loudly proclaimed the superiority of his noble birth and royal descent, and was already, illegally, quartering the royal arms with his own. He boldly asserted that when Henry died, Norfolk would be regent. These rash sentiments led to a quarrel between Surrey and the king's favourite, Sir George Blagge. At about the same time the earl also ran foul of Sir Richard Southwell, a member of the Council. It was almost certainly as a result of Howard intrigue that both these gentlemen found themselves in prison before the summer was out.

Gardiner and his colleagues, thus, had six months during which they could grasp the initiative in framing and implementing policy and they made the most of their opportunity. This was apparent to the imperial ambassador who, analyzing the position towards the end of 1546, could report:

> Affairs here change almost daily. Four or five months ago was great persecution of heretics and sacramentaries, which has ceased since Hertford and the Lord Admiral have resided at court.[77]

Just how mutable, even fickle, official religious policy was becoming is illustrated by two sets of highly confidential royal initiatives taken in August. Henry engaged in discussion with one Gurone Bertano, the first emissary from the Vatican to be allowed into England since the break with Rome. Those privy to this meeting allowed themselves to hope for a rapprochement with the papacy. However, days later, on the arrival of Admiral Claude d'Annebaut, the envoy sent to sign the French peace treaty, the king seriously discussed with him the possibility of France and England both embracing further reforms, including replacing the mass with a new-style communion service. Neither of these mooted innovations came to anything, but it is not difficult to imagine how both Catholic and evangelical partisans must have been alarmed by a state of affairs in which it seemed that everything was up for grabs.

However, we should be careful not to see the "heresy problem" as the only one fuelling discord at the council table. The members faced a daunting series of problems, of which religious disunity was only one. The maintenance of external peace and internal social stability as well as hauling the economy out of the abyss were all major items on their political agenda. And they were all interrelated. To the conservatives it was self-evident that good relations with Charles V would provide the best guarantee of peace and enable the government to concentrate on the nation's internal problems. A firm line with heretics would reassure the emperor, who was

---

77   *L & P*, XXI, pt. ii, 605.

constantly being pressured by Rome to force England back into the Catholic fold. As long as radical religion was being encouraged by people in high places, the wrong message was being sent out. Evangelicals were in a strong position, not only in the king's inner sanctum but also in the House of Commons which was displaying a worrying tendency to baulk anti-reformist motions sent down from the upper house. If Gardiner and his supporters were to set the tide of policy running in the right direction they had to act boldly and even take risks. And they did not know how long they had to establish their ascendancy. Time was of the essence. The question uppermost in all minds – the one nobody dared speak in public – was, "When will the king die?" The moment Henry VIII breathed his last, political power would revert to the Council, who would rule in the name of the underage Edward VI. This explains the increase in tempo of action against prominent evangelicals in the middle months of 1546.

The conservative onslaught began in May, with further examinations of the evangelical celebrity Dr Edward Crome of St Mary Aldermary. He had disclaimed sacramentarian tendencies but not in language vigorous enough to satisfy the establishment. He was thus ordered to make a fuller recantation at St Paul's Cross. While the preacher considered his position, several friends urged him to remain firm. Foremost among these bold counsellors was John Lascelles. Others were Robert Huick, the king's physician; John Taylor, Vicar of St Bride's; one of several priests exiled from Scotland by the regent, Mary of Guise; and a young court page by the name of Worley. Crome's resolve was strengthened by the promptings of his co-religionists and his declaration at Paul's Cross on 9 May was, from the Catholic point of view, quite inadequate. He read to the congregation the statement of orthodox doctrine prepared for him but afterwards added that "he came not thither to recant nor to deny his words nor would not".[78]

The representatives of the Council who had attended the sermon to satisfy themselves that their wishes were carried out

---

78 Strype J. *Ecclesiastical Memorials of the Church of England*, 1823, III, i, p. 160.

wasted no time. Crome was arrested again and re-examined by the Council the next day. A body of learned theologians was called in to assist the councillors. This group included Nicholas Ridley (Bishop of Rochester), Bonner, Nicholas Heath (Bishop of Worcester), William May (Dean of St Paul's), John Redman (Master of Trinity, Cambridge), and Doctors Robinson and Fox (both prominent canon lawyers who assisted with most of the doctrinal formularies drawn up in Henry's reign and his son's).

Crome had played into the hands of his adversaries. He was now in danger of the fire. Recantation was not sufficient. It was made clear that, if he wished to save himself, he must provide the Council with the names of others who shared his beliefs. At first Crome stood firm, but after a sleepless night in prison he broke down before the Council. Names were wrung from him and Gardiner's friends swung into action immediately. That same day (11 May) the jubilant, but cautious bishops wre able to report to the Council secretary:

> As it appears that sundry persons have used themselves with Crome otherwise than is tolerable, the writers would know the King's pleasure (being loth to offend either by doing too much or too little), and have again the depositions and examinations. Crome notes that he was also comforted by one Lascelles, whom they are examining, not upon Crome's detection, but because he boasted a desire to be called to the Council. Dr Huick, the physician, appearing this day upon a complaint made against him, in the variance with his wife, the writers take the opportunity to examine him also, and will send his answers ... these cumbersome matters have consumed much time.[79]

The repercussions of Crome's confession were felt throughout the realm:

79　*L & P*, XXI, pt. i, 740.

> This Doctor Crome, after his committing, while he was
> in the ward at Greenwich, in the court under my Lord
> Chancellor, accused divers persons as well of the court as of
> the city, with other persons in the country, which put many
> persons to great trouble, and some suffered death after.[80]

The round-up of notable Protestants in the city gathered momentum. On 13 May, the Council reported, "This day we look for Latimer, the Vicar of St Bride's, John Taylor, and some others that have specially comforted Crome in his folly.[81] Hugh Latimer had to submit to long and repeated examinations before the Council and angered his examiners by his prevarication. Having failed to discover his real opinions ("to fish out the bottom of his stomach", as they described it), or to implicate him with Crome's heresy, they committed the ex-bishop to the Tower.

Gardiner was much too busy with the courtiers who had been arrested to bother about Hugh Latimer, whose influence had much diminished since his departure from London in 1539. On 14 May, Dr Huick was examined. The Council had two matters to investigate. Huick had recently turned his wife out of doors (an action for which he claimed the king's support). Then there was the issue of his alleged heresy. Quickly leaving the matrimonial matter behind, they went on to consider the doctor's religious opinions. Huick was as outspoken as usual about his beliefs and it is no surprise to learn that he was committed to ward to await further examination.[82]

Now it was the turn of John Lascelles. Quite how he became involved is not clear. From Gardiner's account it would seem that he had boasted of his views, either because he felt sure of the king's support or because he really wished to court martyrdom. Under close and repeated questions the member of the Privy Chamber refused to commit himself on matters of doctrine and

---

80 Wriothesley C. A. *Chronicle of England*, Camden Society, Second Series, 1875, p. 16.

81 *L & P*, XXI, pt. i, 810.

82 *L & P*, XXI, pt. i, 82–3.

claimed his master's protection. This drew forth a wry comment from Gardiner in his report:

> Lascelles will not answer that part of his conference
> with Crome which touches Scripture without the
> King's command and his protection, saying that it is
> neither wisdom nor equity to kill himself. Thus the
> King must pardon before he know, if Mr Lascelles
> may have his will.[83]

John Lascelles was apparently confident that the king would come to his aid (a confidence which Gardiner, obviously, did not share). His attitude throughout his examinations was obstinate. He never deviated from what he believed to be the truth and, when he saw that he could expect no help from the king, he willingly confessed his heresies and faced the consequences. The next day, 15 May, he and his colleagues (Huick and Worley) were examined again and still proved obdurate. Two others appeared slightly more tractable:

> The vicar of St Bride's shows himself of the same sort,
> but not so bold. The Scot is more meet for Dunbar than
> London ... he will say whatever is required of him to get off.[84]

By 17 May the Council had had enough of examining heretics:

> Business – Doctor Huick, Lascelles, the Scottish priest,
> Worley ... for erroneous opinions and dissuading Crome
> from his promise in the declaration of the articles, were
> committed to the Tower ...[85]

The hunt for heretics was swiftly taken up beyond the capital. On 15 May, Bonner, who had wasted no time in holding Six Articles commissions in his diocese, reported to the king that four men and

---

83 *L & P*, XXI, pt. i, 82.
84 *L & P*, XXI, pt. i, 82.
85 *L & P*, XXI, pt. i, 848.

one woman had been found guilty of heresy in Essex and wished to know if public example might be made of them. Henry's prompt reply revealed that he was still unprepared to instigate a large-scale persecution. He ordered that two men, who had repented, were to be released. The remainder were to be burned at Colchester and two other places – but, unless "a general infection" was apparent or any others were "notably detected", the commissioners were to dissolve their assembly "until a more commodious time". It was on 15 May also that the justices of the peace in Suffolk arrested one John Kirby on suspicion of sacramental heresy. On the same day a priest at Tenterden in Kent was sent up to the Council for uttering "a lewd sermon".[86]

While the king was cautious about burning people, he was more easily persuaded to burn books. A new proclamation against heretical literature was issued and Bonner supervised bonfires at St Paul's Cross in July and September. England was now experiencing the most extensive religious persecution since the attack on the monasteries. As their activities went unchecked by the king, the conservative bloodhounds became bolder, turning their attention to people who had been examined earlier and released. Ex-Bishop Shaxton was summoned from his parish at Hadleigh in Suffolk. Shaxton had clearly beaten a diplomatic retreat when things began to "hot up" in London, but his exit had not been swift enough. Despite his gesture in 1539, he was not the stuff that martyrs are made of. His examinations and recantation in 1546 broke him utterly and he never returned to the Protestant fold. He ended his days as a minor persecutor under Queen Mary.

On 24 May, two yeomen of the chamber were sent to fetch Robert Wisdom an incorrigible preacher of reform who had had an earlier run-in with Bonner and had been living in Staffordshire for the last three years.[87] As soon as he heard that the Council's interest in him had revived, Wisdom fled. Within days he was

---

86   *L & P*, XXI, pt. i, 835, 836, 845, 790.

87   For a clear examination of the troubled career of Robert Wisdom, see Bailey S. "Robert Wisdom under Persecution, 1541–1543", in *Journal of Ecclesiastical History*, II:ii, 2011, pp. 180ff.

safely in Flanders. He was not alone. By late summer a diplomat could report from the Low Countries:

> About 60 Englishmen are fled over here for fear of death
> ... so that here are tales of persecution by the bishops,
> and the king is slandered for suffering it. These things are
> spoken by the best in the land.[88]

The two charged with apprehending Wisdom had another errand to perform; they "had with them letters to one Kyme and his wife for their appearance within ten days after receipt".[89]

In March, Bishop Bonner had been only too happy to see the back of the disrespectful, Bible-quoting gospeller. He knew well about her friends and supporters at court but was too circumspect to make capital out of Anne's connections in the royal entourage. A mere two months later the situation was very different. To discover what happened when the court officers reached Lincolnshire we are reliant on local legends and an account written in 1607 by her nephew, Sir Edward Ayscough (as the name was then spelled), *A Historie containing the Warres Treaties Marriages and other occurents between England and Scotland, from King William the Conqueror until the happy Union of them both in our gracious King James.* Anne was under the protection of her brother. Thus, the men from Westminster drew a blank when they arrived at her husband's home in Friskney and presented their warrant. Kyme was only too ready to co-operate and accompanied them to South Kelsey. Messages were also sent to Lincoln requesting the bishop's men to join them there.

Sir Francis, hoping his position would protect both him and his sister from interference, kept Anne at home until he received word that she was in danger. By that time, it was too late to send her very far for refuge and she was hidden in a cottage fairly close at hand. Sir Francis may well have reflected as the bishop's men dismounted in his courtyard that it was almost exactly ten years since that other

---

88 *L & P*, XXI, pt. i, 1491.
89 *L & P*, XXI, pt. i, 898.

occasion when Catholic zeal had forced its way into South Kelsey Hall. In October 1536, he had been the quarry and it is impossible that he can have forgotten the fear and panic of being pursued by men full of a hatred inspired by religion. He knew not only how desperate was Anne's plight if she were captured; he knew just how she felt. So he and his wife were circumspect in responding to the questions and threats of the searchers.

They might have succeeded in their subterfuge had the investigators not managed to intercept a note Anne had sent to her brother. Now the bishop's officers realized that Squire Askew knew his sister's whereabouts. Francis was in a cruel dilemma, as the family chronicler pointed out when he wrote up the episode years afterwards:

> Mine aunt Anne, after many threats and great search
> made for her by the prelates her persecutors, was by
> casual intercepting of her own letter discovered, and so
> unwillingly delivered into their bloody hands, by him, that
> both loved her and the religion which she professed, but
> was never the less overcome with fear (for he had much to
> lose) lest haply by concealing what was known he knew, he
> might so have brought himself into trouble. Thus much
> flesh and blood prevailed with him, which often had such
> power even over the most regenerate, that the Apostle Paul
> saith of himself, "what I would that I do not; but what I
> hate even that I do".[90]

According to the most colourful local story, when Anne learned that her arrest was imminent, she took her copy of Tyndale's New Testament, wrapped it in some bread dough she had been kneading and thrust it into the cottage's brick oven. Then she fled into Kelsey woods. Here it was that she was discovered. From the fact that she was never charged with being in possession

---

90   Ayscough, E. *A Historie containing the Warres Treaties Marriages and other occurents between England and Scotland, from King William the Conqueror until the happy Union of them both in our gracious King James*, 1607, pp. 105ff.

of heretical literature it would seem that her New Testament escaped detection.

Having at last laid hands on her who was legally his wife, Thomas Kyme hastened to London with her. Sir Francis Askew was left behind, suffering, if the family historian is to be believed, terrible pangs of remorse – and worse:

> From the time he had left her with them, till the hour
> wherein she suffered, a flame of fire presented itself
> in the day time to view such (as according to his own
> comparison) appeareth in a glass window over against a
> great fire in the same room. Doubtless this sign was given
> to him to some end, and I doubt not, but he made good
> use thereof.[91]

Meanwhile, Gardiner, Wriothesley, Rich, and their agents had been feverishly active. Latimer, Shaxton, Lascelles, and others were still in prison and others were on the point of being detained. On 29 May, Robert Huick's case came up for review again and he was bound over on recognizance until Michaelmas. On 7 June, more minor figures at court were apprehended: "Weston the luteplayer for conferences with Barker, Latham, Lascelles and others upon prophecies and other things stirring to commotion against the King's Majesty committed to the Porter's Lodge."[92] The depositions of these men, which were considered two days later, reveal Latham to have been more mad than heretical and Weston little more than rather foolish and unguarded in his speech. That the Council bothered with them at all reveals the extent of their vigilance at this time.

Richard Rich now attempted to net bigger fish. William Morice was a gentleman usher to the king and the father of Archbishop Cranmer's secretary, Ralph Morice. The latter held a key position among the group of nobles and gentlemen opposed to the Norfolk/Gardiner/Wriothesley/Rich faction. On more than

---

91   Ayscough 1607, p. 89.
92   *L & P*, XXI, pt. i, 1013.

one occasion he had used his influence to help those attacked on heresy charges. Clearly Morice's father was in a position to give valuable information to his accusers and as a hostage might prove valuable in a number of ways. Yet some contemporaries who well understood Baron Rich's devious mind were not above suggesting another motive for his attack on Morice: that gentleman had valuable lands at Chipping Ongar, sufficiently near Rich's own Essex estates to make them particularly attractive to the councillor.

The other courtier accused by Rich was Sir Richard Southwell. His religious beliefs cannot be considered as anything other than orthodox (indeed he later proved himself an enthusiastic persecutor of Protestants under Mary Tudor) but he was one of those men of comparatively humble origin who had been raised to positions of influence and usefulness by Cromwell. He was another member of the anti-Howard party and had but recently quarrelled with the Earl of Surrey. In the court of the ailing king, religious differences, political disputes and personal rivalries were mingling to create a "dog eat dog" situation. Heresy was as good a charge as any other to bring against someone one wanted out of the way, and it was a good deal easier to prove than many other charges. In that intellectually exciting age, most educated men had bought or read banned books and listened to heretical sermons at some time or other.

On 19 June, Mr and Mrs Kyme appeared before the Council. Ostensibly, they were there in connection with their marital dispute but this was soon waived aside in order that the real reason for Anne's apprehension could be pursued:

> For that she was very obstinate and heady in reasoning of matters of religion, wherein she avowed herself to be of a naughty opinion, seeing no persuasions of good reasons could take place, she was sent to Newgate to remain there to answer to the law.[93]

---

93   Dasent J. R. (ed.) *Acts of the Privy Council of England Volume 1, 1542–1547*, London, 1890, p. 462.

But not before she had been harangued by the Council for four hours after her husband's dismissal. They got straight to the point: what was Anne's belief about the sacrament of the altar? Her answer reads like a prepared statement – which is almost certainly what it was:

> I believe that so oft as I, in a Christian congregation, do
> receive the bread, in remembrance of Christ's death, and
> with thanksgiving, according to his holy instruction, I receive
> therewith also the fruits of his most glorious passion.

This was a positive attempt to state a belief which agreed with the words of institution while avoiding the question of Christ's presence in the elements.

Not unnaturally, Gardiner considered her reply mere prevarication. Did she or did she not accept the doctrine of transubstantiation? Anne refused to elaborate on her statement. What her inquisitors failed to grasp was that the woman they were now dealing with was not the same woman who had faced Bonner only a few weeks before. In March she had recanted her sacramentarianism – or, at least, she had set her name to a statement the bishop claimed as a recantation. The word had been deliberately put about that this evangelical celebrity had abandoned her beliefs. Her apostasy (or apparent apostasy) must have occasioned Anne great remorse. She felt deeply that reports of her denial of the truth had been a blow to her brothers and sisters in the faith. She would not allow the same thing to happen again. Crome, Shaxton, and others might fall into the sin of backsliding; she would not. She was resolved to stand by the Gospel, as she understood it – whatever the cost. From the moment of her third arrest she had become a martyr in her own mind. If she was called upon to go to the stake she would do so, knowing beyond all doubt that a few minutes' pain would be but the threshold to an eternity of bliss. This was something her accusers did not realize and the mistake would undermine their entire strategy. They were getting steadily closer to the centre of power. The king had raised no protest at Lascelles's arrest and now one of his Privy Chamber favourites, George Blagge, joined Lascelles in the Tower.

All this was very worrying to the friends of reform and when Anne was brought back to the Council chamber for another bout of questioning (on 20 or 21 June) it may well have been those sympathetic to her who suggested a more friendly approach. She was taken into an antechamber where William Parr and John Dudley joined Bishop Gardiner, to try their arts of persuasion. Once again Anne was urged to confess that the Sacrament was "flesh, blood, and bone". Far from being cowed, Anne carried the attack into the enemy camp:

> Then said I to my Lord Parr and my Lord Lisle that it was a great shame for them to counsel contrary to their knowledge.[94]

It has usually been suggested that Parr and Dudley, as Anne suggested, were being hypocritical, but there is no reason to believe that, at this stage, either of them had embraced sacramentarianism. As we have seen, the queen's writings did not indicate extremist views about the sacrament and even Cranmer was yet to reject the old doctrine of the mass. If, as has been suggested, the religion espoused by Catherine Parr and the members of her chamber fell well short of Zwinglianism or Anabaptism they had nothing to fear from their enemies. What they did have to fear was the charge of aiding and abetting sacramentaries. This is why the queen's brother and Lady Dudley's husband were anxious to give the impression of being on the side of orthodoxy. They also knew that, once condemned, Anne would be pressed to name her supporters, thus giving their enemies the excuse to examine members of the queen's entourage. Anne's obduracy denied them this escape route. All they could do was tell the prisoner (perhaps *sotto voce*) "that they would gladly all things were well".[95]

The next to try to reason with the prisoner was William Paget,

---

94   Beilin E. V. (ed.) *The Examinations of Anne Askew*, Oxford, 1996, p. 96.
95   Beilin 1996, p. 96.

the king's secretary. He was one of Gardiner's protégés but being skilled at testing the prevailing wind, he was moving towards the Seymour–Dudley caucus. He offered Anne politician's advice: "Tell me what you really believe; you can always deny it later." That suggestion received short shrift. Paget went on to ask how Anne could possibly deny the plain words of Christ "This is my body, which shall be broken for you."

> I answered, that Christ's meaning was, as in other places of the Scriptures: "I am the door" (John 10), "I am the vine" (John 15), "Behold the Lamb of God" (John 1), "The rock-stone was Christ" (1 Corinthians 10) and such other like. Ye may not here, said I, take Christ for the material thing he is signified by; for then ye will make him a very door, a vine, a lamb, and a stone, clean contrary to the Holy Ghost's meaning. All these, indeed, do signify Christ, like as the bread doth his body in that place. And though he did say there, "Take, eat this in remembrance of me"; yet did he not bid them hang up that bread in a box, and make it a God, or bow to it.[96]

Paget's argument was one that any good Lutheran might have offered. On the sacrament Luther clung doggedly to the actual words of Scripture. While rejecting the Aristotelian speculation about "substance" and "accidents" in the sacred elements, Luther refused to depart from the plain words of Christ – "This is my body ... this is my blood".

Anne's examination went on for the next few days against a background of spectacular advance by the forces of reaction. Crome's much-publicized humiliation occurred on 27 June as a London merchant reported to his brother abroad:

> Our news here of Doctor Crome's canting, recanting, decanting or rather double-canting, be these: that on Sunday last, before my Lord Chancellor, the Duke of Norfolk,

---

96   Beilin 1996, p. 99.

my Lord Great Master, Mr Rich, Mr Chancellor of the Tenths, with the Southwells, Pope, and other nobles and knights; and on the other side the Bishops of London and Worcester, all principal doctors and deans, besides the city fathers and a rabble of other marked people. The reverent father first-named openly declared his true meaning and right understanding (as he said, according to his conscience) of the six or seven articles you heard of, as he should have done upon the second Sunday after Easter, but that he was kept from his said true intent by the persuasions of certain perverse-minded persons, and by the sight of lewd and ungodly books and writings, for the which he was very sorry, and desired the audience to beware of such books, for under the fair appearance of them was hid a dangerous encumbrance of Christian consciences … so he exhorted all men to embrace ancientness of Catholic doctrine and forsake newfangledness.[97]

We might reasonably speculate whether Anne was brought the short distance from Newgate to St Paul's to hear Crome's volte-face. It would seem to have been too good an opportunity for her opponents to miss.

Their other activity continued behind the scenes. William Morice was bound over for a year on recognizances. The Council records also note the examination of other, unspecified, persons for heresy – some of whom were glad to be dismissed with a caution. On 19 June, the Council examined Christopher Wright, a merchant, "who attempted to make an erroneous book". He was packed off to Newgate after showing himself of "a wrong opinion concerning the Blessed Sacrament".[98] On 23 June, Mr Lucas of Colchester, one of the commissioners for the Six Articles, hampered by the king's command not to be overzealous in prosecuting offenders, sent up to be examined by the Council one John Hadlam, a tailor of Essex.

---

97   Henry Ellis, *Original Letters*, Second Series, Volume II, p. 176; C. Wriothesley 1875, I, pp. 166–67.

98   Dasent, 1890, I, p. 462.

He was interviewed at Greenwich the same day and was found to be obstinate. He was allowed time to consider his position and re-examined. Proving quite truculent, he was then sent to Newgate.[99] In Norwich, the bishop acting, according to Foxe, in concert with the Duke of Norfolk, had one Rogers arrested and sent to London and to the flames.[100]

On 28 June, Anne was brought to the Guildhall for her formal trial by the quest. She was not alone. "Quondam Bishop Shaxton, mistress Askew, Christopher White … and a tailor that came from Colchester or thereabouts [ie. Hadlam], were arraigned at the Guildhall and received their judgement of the Lord Chancellor and the Council …" The picture of an ex-bishop, a merchant, a tailor, and a gentlewoman being tried together for heresy provides a graphic illustration of the extent to which the new ideas were spreading at all levels of society. Sometime during the previous week, Anne had written down and submitted to the Council her ideas concerning the Lord's Supper and it was on the basis of this that she was tried.

Anne and her three fellows stood before the members of the Council in the lofty Guildhall where Anne had first been put on trial just over a year before. The tailor, the merchant, and the ex-bishop were all found guilty and condemned to be burned. Anne's inquisition is best told in her own words:

> They said to me there, that I was a heretic, and condemned
> by the law, if I would stand in mine opinion. I answered,
> that I was no heretic, neither yet deserved I any death by the
> law of God. But as concerning the faith which I uttered and
> wrote to the Council, I would not, I said, deny it because
> I knew it true. Then would they needs to know if I would
> deny the Sacrament to be Christ's body and blood. I said,
> "Yes," for the same Son of God, who was born of the
> Virgin Mary, is now glorious in heaven, and will come again
> from thence at the latter day like as he went up. [101]

---

99   Dasent, 1890, I, p. 464.

100   Foxe J. *Acts and Monuments*, Volume V, p. 553.

101   Foxe J. *Acts and Monuments*, Volume V, p. 546.

After such an outspoken declaration, there could be no question of an acquittal. And so sentence was passed – death by burning. The court rose – the Catholic councillors withdrawing to continue their efforts to bring down their opponents, the prisoners being escorted to Newgate to meditate on the fiery ordeal before them. For two of them the prospect proved too terrifying: Shaxton and White recanted during the next few days and were assured of the king's pardon.

For Anne this should have been the end of her investigation but simply to burn her would not have served the purpose of her adversaries. In fact, it could only have been counterproductive, for her case had roused great sympathy. We cannot but be struck by the enormous lengths to which the Catholic party went in order to extract a recantation from this one young woman. In their eyes she was obviously a very important part of their campaign. Now they brought her out of her dank prison cell to a private room at the sign of the Crown, a brewhouse in nearby Warwick Lane. The psychology behind this change of location was presumably directed at relaxing the prisoner in the hope that she might drop her guard. At the Crown she suffered a further round of questioning by Bishop Bonner. This time he was assisted by the most sinister member of the conservative caucus, Richard Rich. This seems to be the first time that he had assumed a leading role in Anne's interrogation. Perhaps he had been concentrating his efforts on more socially elevated evangelicals. Gardiner and Bonner did what they did largely out of religious conviction. Rich was nothing more than a self-serving politique. This expert in destroying reputations (and profiting materially in the process) was, as we have seen, targeting various court personalities and it is significant that, from this point, he ruthlessly increased the pressure on his hapless victim. It was he who now brought in someone else to try his powers of persuasion. This was the turncoat ex-bishop Nicholas Shaxton. It would seem that he managed to say only a few words before feeling the edge of Anne's tongue: "I said to him that it would have been good for him never to have been born, with many other like words."[102]

---

102   Beilin 1996, p. 119.

From this point Rich took over. He sent her immediately to the royal prison of the Tower of London. In the secret precincts within its formidable walls he would be able to go beyond convention and beyond the law in using Anne Askew to further his plans against leading evangelicals – and, in particular, Queen Catherine.

CHAPTER 10

Instant Desire

T he crisis was about to wrap its tentacles around the Queen of England. We have no precise date for the attack made by Gardiner and his colleagues and only one source that provides the details of what has become a well-known story. John Foxe recorded it immediately after his account of the persecution of Anne Askew and her fellow sufferers and stated that Catherine Parr's crisis occurred "about the same time".[103] Some historians have rejected it, however, without cogent evidence for doing so. Certainly it dovetails very neatly into the wider story of the religious troubles of the summer of 1546 and historians are always wary of snugly fitting evidence. However, all the players in this palace drama are readily recognizable from what we already know about them and the main events are echoes of ones that had happened before in the turbulent court politics of Henry VIII's reign.

This king had displayed an inclination verging on the psychotic to dispose of those close to him. Four of his previous five wives had been rejected (two of them murdered) as had his three closest advisers: Wolsey, More, and Cromwell. Those who wanted to break the evangelical movement by destroying its most exalted advocate, Catherine Parr, might very reasonably have concluded that Henry would not hesitate to get rid of her if the mood took him. The king's monumental self-belief often led him to make far-reaching decisions based on a sudden whim and this tendency had increased as pain played havoc with his temper. Added to this was his long-standing interest in theology. Henry's doctrinal beliefs

---

103   The story appears in *Acts and Monuments*, V, pp. 553ff.

changed over the years, rendering it difficult for observers to keep up with him. Yet, he was always convinced that what he believed at any particular time was absolute orthodoxy, and he had a genuine abhorrence of heresy. If he could be persuaded that religious untruth had penetrated to the most private quarters of the royal precincts then he might well lend his support to the kind of purge Gardiner and others were pinning their hopes on.

"He might"! There was always an element of risk in pushing Henry to extremes. The well-tested policy for bringing down prominent royal servants was to suggest to Henry that the beliefs and behaviour of the chosen target merited investigation. Once Henry's assent to this had been given, the unfortunate victim was whisked off to the Tower, out of sight and out of the king's mind. His/her doom was sealed. Only if the prisoner could obtain a personal interview with Henry or, failing that, could get some of Henry's intimates to appeal on his/her behalf, might the inevitable process of condemnation be halted. Personal considerations weighed more heavily with Henry than issues of principle. This is why, for example, John Lascelles insisted on explaining his beliefs to the king. He failed to gain the required royal audience. However, his Privy Chamber colleague, George Blagge, did persuade advocates to plead his case to the king and this led to his immediate release from the Tower. On two previous occasions the enemies of reform had launched attacks on the principal agents of reform – Cranmer and Cromwell. The latter had been a spectacular success. The former had been an equally spectacular failure. Would they take the risk of trying to turn the king against his queen?

Gardiner may have been goaded by personal grievance. He had suffered various slights at the hands of Catherine and her boon companions. The appeal made by Cambridge University in connection with the Chantries Act[104] was sent to the queen in the name of the chancellor and vice-chancellor of the university. And who was the chancellor? Stephen Gardiner. It must have irked him, one of the leading academics of the day, to go cap-in-hand to a mere woman. The evangelical sermonette Catherine sent in reply

104   See, p. 121.

must have been hard to take. The bishop was something of a hate figure in the queen's apartments. As we have seen, he was the butt of many jokes, including the standing insult of the Duchess of Suffolk being followed everywhere by her pet spaniel, "Gardiner". Whatever standing he enjoyed with the king, the bishop was well aware that he was not much loved in the inner sanctum of the royal couple. This unpopularity extended to the household of the young prince. Catherine had taken a lead in choosing Edward's tutors and had been careful to see that he was surrounded by reformist humanists of the stamp of Roger Ascham, John Cheke, and Anthony Cooke.

But the bishop had one very specific reason for animosity towards the queen. A year previously, when arrangements were being made for the government during the king's absence in France, Catherine had been named as regent. A small committee was nominated to assist her. The Bishop of Winchester was not included on this body (whose principal members were Cranmer, Seymour, and Wriothesley). Whether the queen played any part in deciding the membership of her council is not known but Gardiner may well have felt himself cold-shouldered by her. The queen and her evangelical clique seemed immovable. Catherine had reconnected her husband with his children and given him the family he had never had. With her friends, Lady Seymour and Lady Dudley, basking in the glory of their husbands' military success, she had formed a non-political but influential group at the centre of national life. It is almost inevitable that Gardiner would be on the alert for any opportunity which might enable him to turn the tide.

If he had known where Catherine's religious meditation was leading he would have been even more alarmed. The book she was working on in 1546 was *The Lamentation of a Sinner*, an intense personal testimony, an account of her own spiritual journey from her blind following of traditional Catholicism to the opening of her eyes to the love of Christ and the salvation that comes from faith, not works. The book was not published until after Henry VIII's death, nor could it have been. The *Lamentation* was spiritual dynamite and, if Gardiner could have got his hands on a draft, the explosion would have destroyed Catherine and many others with her. It was eventually published in a much-altered spiritual atmosphere and, as the author stated, at the "instant desire" of her brother, William Parr, and her best friend, Catherine Brandon.[105] This book was in a similar vein to Margaret of Navarre's *Mirror of the Sinful Soul*, which Princess Elizabeth had translated for her step-mother in 1544, but Catherine's spiritual manual was personal, original, and owed much less to earlier writings than her former books. If *Lamentation* represents Catherine's most pressing thoughts in the summer of 1546, clearly she was spiritually straining at the leash to be free of the restraints of England's official religion.

The text begins with a grovelling confession which is also a denunciation of conventional Catholicism:

> When I consider, in the bethinking of mine evil
> and wretched former life, mine obstinate, stony, and
> untractable heart to have so much exceeded in evilness
> that hath not only neglected, yea, contemned and
> despized God's holy precepts and commandments, but
> also embraced, received, and esteemed vain, foolish,
> and feigned trifles: I am, partly by the hate I owe to sin,
> who hath reigned in me, partly by the love I owe to all
> Christians, whom I am content to edify, even with the
> example of mine own shame, forced and constrained with
> my heart and words to confess and declare to the world,
> how ingrate, negligent, unkind, and stubborn I have been
> to God my Creator; and how beneficial, merciful, and
> gentle He hath been always to me, His creature, being such
> a miserable and wretched sinner.[106]

Catherine goes on to confess that she adhered to superstition and "little regarded God's word". Led by ignorance she recalls that she walked with the multitude.

---

105 Interestingly, John Bale used a similar expression when he published Anne Askew's account of her trials. He undertook the task, as he explained, "at the instant desire of certain faithful men and women".
106 Mueller 2011, p. 447.

I could not think but I walked in the perfect and right way, having more regard to the number of the walkers than to the order of the walking, believing also most surely with company to have walked to heaven, whereas I am most sure they would have brought me down to hell.[107]

When we set these words in their historical context it is impossible not to connect the queen's remorse with the persecution being suffered by those who were being imprisoned and burned for their faith – and, surely, Anne Askew would have been uppermost in her mind. The girl Catherine had heard of and, perhaps, met as a lively teenager in Lincolnshire was now boldly upholding her faith, with her eyes fixed on martyrdom while she, the queen, lived in luxury, hoping that Anne's interrogation would not lead the Catholic bloodhounds to her door.

Catherine walked the path that Luther and countless others had trodden from utter despair at their sinfulness and alienation from God to the realization that only faith justifies them and that it is only made possible by God's prevenient grace (that is, the disposition that allows them to accept Christ's finished work on their behalf). Here we see, unequivocally, Catherine's embracing of Bible-based faith and it is worth quoting her words *in extenso*:

I never had this unspeakable and most high charity and abundant love of God printed and fixed in my heart duly, till it pleased God, of his mere grace, mercy and pity, to open mine eyes, making me to see and behold with the eye of lively faith, Christ crucified to be mine only Saviour and Redeemer. For then I began (and not before) to perceive and see mine own ignorance and blindness; the cause thereof was that I would not learn to know Christ, my Saviour and Redeemer. But when God, of His mere goodness, had thus opened mine eyes, and made me see and behold Christ, the wisdom of God, the Light of the world, with a supernatural sight of faith: all pleasures,

---

107   Mueller 2011, p. 449.

vanities, honour, riches, wealth, and aids of the world
began to wax bitter unto me. Then I knew it was no
illusion of the devil, nor false nor human doctrine I had
received, when such success came thereof: that I had in
detestation and horror, that which I previously so much
loved and esteemed, being of God forbidden, that we
should love the world or the vain pleasures and shadows
in the same. Then began I to perceive that Christ was my
only Saviour and Redeemer, and the same doctrine to be all
divine, holy, and heavenly, infused by grace into the hearts
of the faithful. Which never can be attained by human
doctrine, wit, nor reason, although they should travail and
labour for the same to the end of the world. Then began
I to dwell in God by charity, knowing by the loving charity
of God, in the remission of my sins, that God is charity, as
Saint John saith.

So that, of my faith (whereby I came to know God, and
thereby it pleased God, even because I trusted in him
to justify me) I think no less, but many will marvel and
wonder at this my saying, that I never knew Christ for
my Saviour and Redeemer until this time. For many have
this opinion, saying, Who knoweth not there is a Christ?
Who, being a Christian, doth not confess Him his Saviour?
And, thus believing their dead, human, historical faith and
knowledge (which they have learned in their scholastical
books) to be the true, infused faith and knowledge of
Christ, which may be had (as I said before) with all sin:
they used to say by their own experience of themselves,
that their faith doth not justify them. And true it is, except
they have this faith, the which I have declared here before,
they shall never be justified. And, yet, it is not false that, by
faith only, I am sure to be justified.[108]

---

108   Mueller 2011, p. 457–59.

With all the reformers Catherine draws the distinction between "historical" or "head" faith and the "heart" faith which justifies. To put it another way believing *about* Christ is not the same thing as trusting *in* Christ.

In the latter part of the book Catherine moves seamlessly from autobiography to exhortation. She warns her readers to avoid the "subtle and crafty persuasions of philosophy and sophistry". Those who would know God must read him in the "spiritual book of the crucifix". She strikes a common chord with most of the reformers in condemning the doctors of the church who claimed to add "unwritten verities" to the plain words of Scripture. In dealing with teachers and preachers her admonition is wide-ranging. While she rejects traditionalists who claim that the study of the Bible leads people into heresy she does not give blanket endorsement to religious radicals. Indeed, in one of the most telling passages of the book, she addresses the problems of divided evangelicalism.

> Now I will speak, with great dolour and heaviness in my heart, of a sort of people which be in the world, that be called "professors of the Gospel", and by their words do declare and show, they be much affected to the same. But, I am afraid, some of them do build upon the sand, as Simon Magus did, making a weak foundation. I mean, they make not Christ their chiefest foundation, professing His doctrine of a sincere, pure, and zealous mind. But either for because they would be called "gospellers" to procure some credit and good opinions of the true and very savourers of Christ's doctrine, either to find out some carnal liberty, either to be contentious disputers, finders, or rebukers of other men's fault, or else, finally, to please and flatter the world: such gospellers are an offense and a slander to the Word of God, and make the wicked to rejoice and laugh at them, saying: Behold, I pray you, their fair fruits. What charity, what discretion, what godliness, holiness, or purity of life is amongst them? Be they not great avengers, foul gluttons, slanderers, backbiters, adulterers, fornicators, swearers, and blasphemers? Yes,

and wallow and tumble in all sins; these be the fruits of
their doctrine. And thus it may be seen how the Word of
God is evil spoken of, through licentious and evil living.[109]

Now we have to ask ourselves an important question, and the
fact that we cannot answer it definitely does not detract from
its importance. Does Catherine include Anne Askew in her
condemnation of licentious radicals? In the accounts of the
martyr's tribulation she was represented as devout and pure in her
private life. She, herself, claimed this, in her exchange with Bonner.
When the bishop observed that many who read the Bible did
not follow its precepts her rebuttal was sharp: "I am so sure of
myself … that there are none able to prove any dishonesty by me.
If you know any that can do it, I pray you bring them forth".[110]
But Catherine had not read Bale's version of events, which was
not available in England until 1547. There were many opinions
about the Lincolnshire gospeller circulating in the capital and the
royal court and we should hesitate before making the assumption
that, because the queen and the heretic were both "Protestants",
Catherine would have given unqualified approval to Anne.

Although they shared the same basic biblical faith, the two
women were markedly different in the application of that faith.
Catherine had resisted her own romantic inclinations when she
accepted Henry's proposal, believing that God was calling her,
for his own purposes, to forego the prospect of connubial bliss.
Anne, by contrast, had abandoned her husband and her children in
order to follow her own desire. Catherine had used her influence
discreetly and accepted the submissive role of a wife as advocated
in Scripture. No one could have called Anne "discreet" or
"submissive". She was far closer to those reproached by the queen
as "contentious disputers" prompted by a lust for "carnal liberty".
Catherine might well have felt herself obliged, "with great dolour
and heaviness" to distance herself from Anne Askew. No less than
the king, she abhorred dissensions and religious conflict. She went

---

109 Mueller 2011, p. 475.
110 Beilin E. V. (ed.) *The Examinations of Anne Askew*, Oxford, 1996, p. 57.

to great lengths to stress the Pauline pattern of social stability. Men
are ordained, she states, to bring up their families:

> in the doctrine of the Lord; in all godliness and virtue,
> committing the instruction of others, which appertaineth
> not to their charge, to the reformation of God and His
> ministers, which chiefly be kings and princes, bearing the
> sword even for that purpose, to punish evildoers. If they be
> children, they honour their father and mother, knowing it to
> be God's commandment, and that He hath thereto annexed
> a promise of long life. If they be servants, they obey and
> serve their masters with all fear and reverence, even for the
> Lord's sake, neither with murmuring nor grudging, but with
> a free heart and mind. If they be husbands, they love their
> wives as their own bodies, after the example as Christ loved
> the congregation, and gave Himself for it, to make it to
> Him a spouse, without spot or wrinkle. If they be women
> married, they learn of Saint Paul, to be obedient to their
> husbands, and to keep silence in the congregation, and to
> learn of their husbands, at home.[111]

However, having said all that, when doctrinal sides have to be taken
she is clear where her sympathies lie and surely the Lincolnshire
martyr cannot have been far from her thoughts when she wrote:

> The children of God be not abashed, although the world
> hate them. They believe they are in the grace and favour
> of God, and that He, as a best Father, doth govern them
> in all things, putting away from them all vain confidence,
> and trust in their own doings. For they know they can do
> nothing but sin, of themselves. They be not so foolish
> and childish, not to give God thanks for their election,
> which was before the beginning of the world. For they
> believe most surely, they be of the chosen: for the
> Holy Ghost doth witness to their spirit that they be the

---

111   Beilin 1996, p. 481.

children of God, and therefore they believe God better than man. They say with Saint Paul: "Who shall separate us from the love of God? Shall tribulation, anguish, persecution, hunger, nakedness, peril, or sword? As it is written: For Thy sake are we killed all day long, and are counted as sheep appointed to be slain. Nevertheless, in all these things, we overcome through Him that loveth us. For I am sure that neither death, neither life, neither angels, nor rule, neither power, neither things present, neither things to come, neither quantity or quality, neither any creature, shall be able to depart us from the love of God, which is in Christ Jesu our Lord." They are not by this godly faith presumptuously inflamed, nor by the same become they loose, idle, or slow in doing of godly works, as carnal men dream of them: so much the more fervent they be in doing most holy and pure works, which God hath commanded them to walk in. They wander not in men's traditions and inventions, leaving the most holy and pure precepts of God undone, which they know they be bound to observe and keep. Also they work not like hirelings for meed [recompense], wages, or reward, but as loving children, without respect of lucre, gain, or hire. They be in such liberty of spirit, and joy so much in God, that their inward consolation cannot be expressed with tongue. All fear of damnation is gone from them, for they have put their whole hope of salvation in His hands, that will and can perform it. Neither have they any post or pillar to lean to, but God and His smooth and unwrinkled Church. For He is to them All in all things, and to Him they lean, as a most sure, square pillar, in prosperity and adversity, nothing doubting of His promises and covenants, for they believe most surely they shall be fulfilled.[112]

---

112   Mueller 2011, pp. 466, 475–79.

We would dearly love to know the precise chronology of the events that occurred in the middle weeks of 1546. Anne was brutally interrogated in the Tower by councillors desperate to drag from her the names of those in the queen's circle who were "of her party". King Henry allowed those same councillors to investigate his wife's religious convictions. Clearly the two events were related. But which came first? Most chroniclers have inclined to the view that Anne's interrogation and, perhaps, her execution predated the assault on the queen. This may be because of the order in which Foxe placed these events. However, as has been mentioned, the martyrologist only said that Catherine Parr's brush with danger took place "about the same time" as Anne's final ordeal. Some have assumed that the attempt on the queen took place after Anne's death because they wanted to make a connection between the queen and a woman who was, beyond any shadow of doubt, a heretic upon whom sentence had been carried out in accordance with the king's justice. But Gardiner, Rich, and Wriothesley had no need to wait until after Anne's death: her heresies were plain to all and she had made no attempt to conceal them. A connection between her and the queen's circle might have been made at any time.

In my view the psychology of the two dramas only makes sense if we assume the move against Catherine came before Anne's ghastly death. "Caesar's wife" was untouchable. The conservative group could not have made a move against her without compelling reason. They would not have dared to manufacture a plot that might have seen the vials of the king's wrath poured out upon them. But then, out of the blue, an opportunity presented itself and they grabbed it eagerly.

Gardiner, as we have seen, had personal, as well as religious reasons for resenting the influence of Catherine and her ladies. The story, as related to Foxe by Anne Parr, Lady Herbert, and others of the queen's chamber, was that the bishop was present one day when Henry and Catherine were discussing religious matters. Given what the queen wrote in her *Lamentation*, it takes no great feat of the imagination to envisage the earnestness with which Catherine entered into the debate. She believed devoutly that God had placed her in such an exalted position so that she could press home evangelical truth. On the occasion in question, Henry had had quite enough of his wife's lecturing and grumbled to Gardiner afterwards that things had come to a pretty pass when men were given lessons in theology by their wives. The quick-witted Gardiner pointed out that the situation was worse than his majesty realized. Some of the teachings being promoted at the queen's regular Bible studies and sermons tended towards Anabaptism, specifically that all property should be held in common among Christians. This was, of course, treason as well as heresy, and Henry, alarmed by the disclosure, agreed to let Gardiner and his colleagues investigate just what was being taught in the queen's quarters.

Did Gardiner really go this far? And, if so, did Henry swallow it? The move against Catherine followed that which had been employed with varying success against Catherine Howard, Thomas Cranmer, and Thomas Cromwell. Study of those examples suggests first, that the king could be manipulated, but second, that he could at any time intervene to short-circuit the train of events. How may we best interpret the plot against the queen and Henry's response? I believe it will be helpful to consider simultaneously events in the Tower and Whitehall.

Anne was taken to the Tower on 29 June. This sudden and unusual move could certainly be explained as part of the investigation of the queen and her circle which had been sanctioned by the king. Certainly Anne's accusers now moved with speed and mounting desperation. At three o'clock that afternoon Richard Rich entered her cell accompanied by "another councillor". This person was identified by Foxe as Sir John Baker, Chancellor of the Exchequer, who had been involved in other heresy investigations, including those connected with the attack on Cranmer in 1543. The motive of the councillors became clear immediately as Anne's account explains:

> They charged me upon my obedience to shew unto them if I knew any man or woman of my sect. My answer was that I knew none.
>
> Then they asked me of my Lady of Suffolk, my Lady of

Sussex, my Lady of Hertford, my Lady Denny, and my Lady Fitzwilliam.

Anne's reply was evasive:

I answered, if I should pronounce anything against them, that I were not able to prove it.

The councillors' next words are significant and appear to confirm the connection between Anne's investigation and events at court.

Then said they unto me that the king was informed that I could name, if I would, a great number of my sect. Then I answered that the king was as well deceived in that behalf as dissembled with in other matters.

It may have been at this point that the Lord Chancellor arrived at the Tower to join his colleagues. Certainly the next questions that Anne was asked turned on information Wriothesley had obtained from his spies months before during Anne's earlier imprisonment.[113]

"Who gave you money when you were in the Counter? Who visited you in prison and urged you to hold firm to your heresies?"

"No one visited me in prison. As to the scant help I received, it came only as a result of my maid's begging the charity of London apprentices in the streets."

"Who were these mysterious and obliging apprentices?"

"I don't know."

"Some of your supporters were not apprentices, but gentlewomen of the court, were they not?"

---

113   From this point I paraphrase in the interests of conciseness.

"They may have been, but if they were I never knew their names."

"We know that some of the ladies of the court sent you money. Who were they?"

"I only know what my maid told me."

"What was that?"

"Once she was given ten shillings by a man in a blue coat. He said it came from Lady Hertford. Another time a servant in violet livery gave her eight shillings, saying that Lady Denny had sent it. That is what my maid told me. I will not swear to its truth."

"Besides these ladies you had help from members of the King's Council, didn't you?"

"No."

The interrogators were making little progress. Yet it was vitally important that they should obtain information against some of the queen's ladies.

The next few hours were crucial. Could Wriothesley and his allies undermine the position of their enemies via their wives? Professor Alec Ryrie does not exaggerate the importance of this little-recognized turning point:

> If Seymour, Dudley, and the queen could have been separated from the king, it would have been a conservative victory comparable with the toppling of Cromwell. Perhaps it would have been greater, since those who were left standing would take charge of the minority government that was plainly approaching.[114]

---

114   Ryrie A. *The Gospel and Henry VIII*, Cambridge, 2003, p. 55.

What Wriothesley did – and what gave rise to public outrage when the news leaked out – was summon the Lieutenant of the Tower, Sir Anthony Knyvett, and order him to have the rack prepared. Knyvett obeyed, apparently with some reluctance, and, when all was ready, Anne was taken to the basement of the White Tower to meet "the Duke of Exeter's daughter", as the instrument was commonly known.

What happened next was something unique in the annals of the Tower of London. Never, in all its one thousand plus years, has any other woman ever been put to the rack. In fact, the use of this implement at all was technically illegal.

Magna Carta had established that "No freeman shall be taken or imprisoned, or disseised, or outlawed or exiled, *or in any way destroyed*, nor will we go upon him, nor will we sent upon him, except by the lawful judgment of his peers or by the law of the land."[115] Later jurists were to affirm that the words italicized comprehended torture, which was never sanctioned by common law. Never sanctioned, that is, if we understand by torture the deliberate infliction of pain upon unconvicted prisoners in order to punish or to extract a confession or to obtain information. The freedom from torture, thus defined, was a right of which Englishmen were very jealous. They prided themselves on not being guilty of the excesses of the Inquisition. Of course, bestial treatment of prisoners did take place and women were among those who suffered it. We need only think of the ducking of witches. But such acts were examples of *public* punishment. The use of *private* torture was not the same thing at all. We might find it hard to see any difference, but our sixteenth-century ancestors certainly made the distinction. When it comes to the use of the Duke of Exeter's daughter, William Blackstone, in his *Commentaries on the Laws of England* (1766), was quite clear on the matter: "trial by rack is utterly unknown to the law of England". As well as being illegal, racking was the subject of social taboos. These outlawed the torture of women and anyone above the rank of yeoman. Of course, the mere existence of the rack means that it was used by

---

115   My italics.

unscrupulous rulers and it was not the only implement employed to make prisoners reveal what the current regime wanted to know; it was simply the biggest. More portable instruments were taken to the prisoners' cells. Bearing all this in mind what were Wriothesley and his aids doing?

My guess is that they found themselves in a situation that got out of hand. They had a royal mandate to find evidence against the queen. Having gained that they wanted to take full advantage of it to achieve their objective; they only needed Anne to give them one or two names. They could then have reported back to Henry, hoping for further permission to clean out the Augean stables of the queen's private quarters. But Anne had proved a tough nut to crack. They needed some other means of loosening her tongue. Probably they hoped that the mere sight of the rack would do the trick. It did not. Therefore, Knyvett had the gaolers strap the prisoner to the machine and turn the screw sufficiently to "pinch" her. Still she refused to answer their questions:

> Because I confessed no ladies nor gentlewomen to be
> of my opinion, thereon they kept me a long time. And
> because I lay still and did not cry, my lord chancellor and
> Master Rich took pains to rack me [with] their own hands,
> till I was nigh dead.[116]

According to Foxe, the lieutenant had dissociated himself from the proceedings. The councillors had personally resumed the torture because he refused to do so and ordered his men to desist also. He immediately set off for Whitehall to report to the king. Meanwhile:

> I sat in long hours reasoning with my lord chancellor upon
> the bare floor, where as he with many flattering words
> [tried to] persuade me to leave my opinion. But my Lord

---

116   Beilin 1996, p. 127.

God (I thank his everlasting goodness) gave me grace to persevere and will do (I hope) to the very end.[117]

When Knyvett reached the palace he gained an audience with the king and reported the councillors' activity. Henry, "seemed not very well to like of their so extreme handling of the woman"[118] – but there is no account anywhere of him taking Wriothesley and Rich to task. They were free to continue with the other part of their investigation, which was to search the queen's chambers for suspicious literature. It is probably no coincidence that the new proclamation against banned books was issued on 8 July. The conservatives must have been reasonably confident that they were keeping the king on side. However, it was as difficult for them to read Henry VIII's mind as it is for us the best part of five centuries later. On 13 July, Lord John Russell, one of the reform-inclined councillors, took the opportunity of his intimacy with the king to secure the release of George Blagge. Other members of the court were active in shielding the queen from danger.

So we come to the dramatic climax to the story of Catherine Parr's brush with danger. Foxe recounted it with relish.[119] Crucially, Catherine became aware of the plot against her by means of a paper listing the charges against her being dropped by a courtier (whether by accident or deliberately we cannot know). She was, understandably, panic-stricken and "fell incontinent into a great

---

117   Beilin 1996, p. 130.

118   Foxe J. *Acts and Monuments*, Volume V, p. 548.

119   Once again we are up against the difficulty of precisely dating crucial events. We know that the attack on the queen occurred while the court was at Whitehall between mid-June and mid-August. Henry had a bad attack of his illness in July but this seems to have cleared by the middle of the month. The burning of Anne and John Lascelles on 16 July was the last execution of high-born heretics and marked the end of the Catholic campaign. By the end of the month, Seymour was back at court more or less permanently. All this suggests a date between 8 July and 25 July for the attempted arrest of the queen, with the likelihood that it occurred earlier within that period.

melancholy and agony, bewailing and taking on in such sort as was lamentable to see". When Henry heard that the queen was ill he sent one of his physicians, Dr Wendy, to tend her. It was Wendy who unfolded to Catherine all the details of the plot.

The queen was not so distracted that she was unable to take action. She immediately ordered her ladies to get rid of all the banned books from her chambers. Then she awaited an opportunity to speak with the king. Late one evening it was reported to her that Henry was in his Privy Chamber talking with a few of his gentlemen and, being less pained with his leg than usual, was in a good mood. Immediately Catherine made her way through the palace complex. Henry received his wife courteously and Catherine wasted little time in unburdening herself. She declared herself completely obedient to her husband and king, who was "so excellent in gifts and ornaments of wisdom" and avowed herself content to be guided by him in all matters of religion.

"Not so, by Saint Mary," replied the king. "You are become a doctor, Kate, to instruct us (as we take it) and not to be instructed or directed by us."

"Kate" replied with appropriate humility:

> If your majesty take it so, then hath your Majesty very much mistaken my intention. For I have ever been of the opinion to think it very unseemly and preposterous for the woman to take on her the office of an instructor or teacher to her lord and husband, but rather to learn of her husband and to be taught by him. And where I have … been bold to hold talk with your Majesty, wherein sometimes in opinions there hath seemed some difference, I have not done it so much to maintain opinion, but … rather to minister talk … to the end your Majesty might with less grief pass over this painful time of your infirmity, being attentive to our talk … and also that I, hearing your Majesty's learned discourse, might receive to myself some profit thereby.

Flattery and abasement worked, as it usually did with Henry. "And is it even so, sweetheart?" the king replied. "And tended your arguments to no worse end? Then perfect friends we are now again, as ever at any time heretofore."

King and queen remained together until far into the night, murmuring endearments to each other while the atmosphere was charged with emotion. But when Catherine at last took her leave with her lord's blessing, the final scene in this little drama had yet to be played.

The following afternoon, king and queen were in the privy garden when Wriothesley arrived with a troop of the royal guard to take Catherine into custody. He did not receive the welcome he had expected. Henry, drawing the councillor to one side, berated him soundly. "Knave! Arrant knave, beast and fool," he chided in a stentorian whisper so loud that the queen heard it. The Chancellor left with his tail between his legs. Catherine's position was permanently secure.[120] The agents of reaction realized that they had gone too far. Reformists in court and Council were in the ascendant for the rest of the reign. It is a good story. But, even if we tone down the martyrologist's penchant for high drama, can we accept it at face value?

The answer depends on what we think was going on in Henry's mind. As so often, that is "a riddle wrapped in a mystery inside an enigma". Did he really contemplate disposing of wife number six? There appears to have been talk around the court that the first fine careless rapture of his relationship with Catherine had worn off but the spat related above is the only concrete evidence of marital rift. If Henry had really been alarmed by Gardiner's revelation, his fear of false religion might have moved him, at least temporarily, to cast the viper of heresy from his bosom. But I believe he saw through Winchester's machinations. He was a shrewd judge of character and he had the bishop's measure. Months later, when plans were being made for a regency council to assist his young son, Henry refused to include Gardiner on the grounds that, while he had always been able to keep the cunning bishop in check, Edward's advisers would not be able to do so. Twice before, Gardiner had tried to deprive his royal master of the services of

---

120   Foxe J. *Acts and Monuments*, Volume V, p. 553–54.

faithful ministers. In the case of Cranmer, Henry had stepped in to snatch him from the jaws of Gardiner and his colleagues. In the case of Cromwell, the king had been bamboozled into sacrificing the minister – and had come to regret being deprived of the "best servant he had ever had" by scheming conciliar rivals.

An explanation of the Catherine Parr affair that fits both Henry's character and the situation might run as follows: the king, an inveterate play actor, pretended to go along with Gardiner's plan. Why? To rap his wife over the knuckles and show her that he was not to be dictated to in matters of religion and to warn everyone that the old, sick lion still had teeth. His actions declared that no one should presume to think that he or she could manipulate Henry Tudor. There was also the wider issue of England's religion. Disunity was a matter of great concern to him, as he had movingly declared in his famous Christmas address to Parliament only a few months before. Even the overweeningly conceited Henry had come to realize that he could not command people's consciences. All he could do was lash out from time to time against religious partisans of either party who had gone too far. In 1546 he sanctioned the fresh outbreak of persecution but he halted the persecutors in their tracks when they presumed too much. On this occasion he kept both sides in court and Council in check. He allowed Catherine and her friends to be threatened and then made sure that they realized what was afoot. He let Gardiner, Wriothesley, and Rich have their head and then abruptly cut them down to size. It was typical of the man.

All this time Anne Askew and John Lascelles remained in Newgate Prison. They occupied themselves not only in prayer, but also in writing messages for other members of their group. Anne wrote a long and detailed account of her two trials which was then smuggled out by her maid and delivered to Anne's friends in the city. Anne's main object in doing this was to counter the official version of her trials which was being published by the Council and particularly the story of her recantation. She also had in mind a friend "not yet thoroughly persuaded in the truth concerning the Lord's Supper, and hoped even from prison to convince him by her exhortation and her example. Neither of the prisoners was allowed to receive visitors but scores of their friends clamoured for news of them and managed by bribery and cunning to get messages into Newgate. Within the prison, Anne and John were even kept apart from each other, but their spirits never faltered. John had suffered less and carried himself throughout his troubles with a flamboyant defiance. Sir George Blagge described how after his condemnation he was in a relaxed and talkative mood. "He mounted up into the window of the little parlour by Newgate and … was merry and cheerful in the Lord … and said these words, 'My Lord Bishop would have me confess the Roman church to be the Catholic church, but that I cannot, for it is not true.'"[121]

Anne, apparently, shared her friend's bravado. When he smuggled her a note of encouragement her response was very upbeat:

> O friend most dearly beloved in God, I marvel not a little what should move you to judge in me so slender a faith as to fear death, which is the end of all misery. In the Lord I desire you not to believe of me such weakness. For I doubt it not but God will perform his work in me, like as he hath begun. I understand the Council is not a little displeased, that it should be reported abroad that I was racked in the Tower. They say now that what they did there was but to frighten me; whereby I perceive they are ashamed of their uncomely doings and fear much lest the King's majesty should have information thereof. Wherefore they do not want any man to tell it abroad. Well, their cruelty God forgive them.
>
> Your heart in Christ Jesus,
>
> Farewell and pray.[122]

---

121 Strype J. *Narratives of the Days of the Reformation*, Volume 77, Cambridge, 1859, p. 148.

122 Foxe J. *Acts and Monuments*, Volume V, p. 549.

Anne was certainly right about the public response. News of her racking was all over London and the overreaction of Wriothesley and Rich was having the opposite effect to that they had intended. So far from discouraging heretics it was making Anne into the heroic martyr she was long to remain.

For her part, she did not run heedlessly to destruction. She made an appeal for pardon to the king, but it was not couched in the grovelling, self-abasing terms to which most Tudor prisoners resorted when pleading for mercy:

> I, Anne Askew, of good memory, although God hath given me the bread of adversity and the water of trouble (yet not so much as my sins have deserved), desire this to be known unto your Grace. Forasmuch as I am by the law condemned for an evil-doer, here I take heaven and earth to record that I shall die in my innocence. And according to what I have said first and will say last, I utterly abhor and detest all heresies. And as concerning the Supper of the Lord, I believe so much as Christ hath said therein, which he confirmed with his most blessed blood. I believe so much as he willed me to follow, and I believe so much as the Catholic church of him doth teach. For I will not forsake the commandment of his holy lips. But ... what God hath charged me with by his mouth, that have I shut up in my heart. And thus briefly I end for lack of learning.[123]

Anne had this delivered to the Lord Chancellor with a covering letter:

> The Lord God, by whom all creatures have their being, bless you with the light of his knowledge. Amen.
>
> My duty to your Lordship remembered, etc. it might please you to accept this my bold suit, as the suit of one which, upon due consideration, is moved to the same and hopeth

---

123   Foxe J. *Acts and Monuments*, Volume V, p. 546.

to obtain. My request to your Lordship is only that it may please the same to be an intermediary for me to the King's Majesty, that his Grace may be certified of these few lines which I have written concerning my belief which, when it shall be truly compared with the hard judgement given me for the same, I think his Grace shall well conceive me to be weighted in an uneven pair of balances. But I remit my matter and cause to Almighty God, who rightly judgeth all secrets. And thus I commend your Lordship to the governance of him, and to the fellowship of all the saints. Amen.[124]

It is unlikely that Anne's suit was ever presented to the king or that it would have availed her had it done so. Others, like Blagge, had influential friends ready to intercede on their behalf. Nicholas Throckmorton, a cousin of the queen, was another who spent an uncomfortable few days in prison before being released at the request of those close to the king. But there was no one to speak up for Anne and John. It would be pleasant to be able to picture Francis Askew rushing up to London and, together with his brother, canvassing support at Westminster for their sister. But there is no evidence and, on the whole, it seems unlikely that Anne's family (or for that matter John Lascelles') were prepared to risk sharing the disgrace of a condemned heretic. Anne had suffered cruel torture of mind and body in protecting the queen and her friends, but they were unwilling or unable to come to her aid.

The last written words Anne left the world took the form of a prayer smuggled out for the edification of her co-religionists:

O Lord, I have more enemies now than there be hairs on my head. Yet, Lord, let them never overcome me with vain words, but fight thou, Lord, in my stead, for on thee cast I my care. With all the spite they can imagine they call upon me, which am thy poor creature. Yet, sweet Lord, let me pay no heed to them which are against me, for in thee

---

124   Foxe J. *Acts and Monuments*, Volume V, p. 546.

is my whole delight. And, Lord, I heartily desire of thee, that thou wilt of thy most merciful goodness forgive them that violence which they do and have done unto me. Open also thou their blind hearts, that they may hereafter do that thing in thy sight, which is only acceptable before thee, and to set forth thy verity aright, without all vain fantasy of sinful man. So be it, O Lord, so be it.[125]

What that "verity" was she set forth succinctly, now that she no longer had need to guard her words carefully:

This is the heresy which they report me to hold, that after the priest hath spoken the words of consecration, there remaineth bread still.

But they both say, and also teach it for a necessary article of faith, that after those words be once spoken, there remaineth no bread, but even the self same body, that hung upon the cross on Good Friday, both flesh, blood and bone. To this belief of theirs say I nay. For then were our common Creed false, which sayeth that he sitteth on the right hand of God the father almighty: And from thence shall come to judge the quick and dead. Lo, this is the heresy that I hold. And for it must suffer the death. But as touching the holy and blessed supper of the Lord, I believe it to be a most necessary remembrance of his glorious sufferings and death. Moreover, I believe as much therein, as my eternal and only redeemer, Jesus Christ would I should believe. Finally I believe all those scriptures to be true, whom he hath confirmed with his most precious blood. Yes, and as S. Paul saith those scriptures are sufficient for our learning and salvation, that Christ hath left here with us. So that I believe, we need no unwritten verities to rule his church with … Some do say, that I deny the *Eucharist* or sacrament of thanksgiving. But

---

125   Beilin 1996, pp. 146–47.

those people do untruely report of me. For I both say and believe it, that if it were ordered, like as Christ instituted it, and left it, a most singular comfort it were unto us all. But as concerning your mass, as it is now used in our days, I do say and believe it, to be the most abominable idol that is in the world. For my God will not be eaten with teeth, neither yet dieth he again. And upon these words, that I have now spoken, will I suffer death.[126]

Whatever influences Anne may have absorbed from native Lollardy or Continental Zwinglianism or Anabaptism, she died as a woman who loved the Bible, understood it simply and, one might say, commonsensically.

Tuesday 16 July was the day fixed for the execution, and the place Smithfield: a large, open space a short walk from Newgate beyond the city wall (though being steadily encroached upon by urban developments), used as a recreation area for citizens. In times past, spectators had gathered there to watch tourneys, but, by 1546, the major attractions there were large cattle and sheep markets, military exercises, the annual St Bartholomew's Fair – and executions. Heretics had ended their days there ever since the first Lollards had suffered early in the fifteenth century, but Londoners had not enjoyed a really good burning since Barnes, Jerome, Garrett, and others had perished in the wake of Cromwell's fall (1540). There can be no doubt that the spectacle attracted a large audience. The woodcut in John Foxe's *Acts and Monuments* depicts a dense crowd packed into the space around the roped-off enclosure surrounding the stakes and the pulpit as well as other watchers enjoying a good view from windows and rooftops. Though dating from seventeen years after the event there is no reason to doubt its accuracy. Nor can it be doubted that the star attraction was Anne Askew. Whether they had come to pray or jeer, everyone wanted to see the woman who had been racked in the Tower and who had to be carried to the execution site on a chair. The arena was dominated by the imposing bulk of the ex-priory church of

---

126   Beilin 1996, pp. 189–90.

St Bartholomew the Great (only recently reopened as a place of worship since the dissolution) and in front of it had been erected a temporary scaffolding covered by an awning. Seated in this prominent position were Wriothesley, the Duke of Norfolk, Lord Russell, other councillors, and the Lord Mayor.

At last the moment arrived that everyone had been waiting for. A path was opened through the throng and John Lascelles, John Hadlam, the Essex tailor, and John Hemsley, an ex-Observant friar, walked in with their armed escort.[127] Anne followed, her chair borne by four guards. But it was not only the sight of the prisoners that silenced the mob. Much to everyone's surprise, the condemned heretics were accompanied by a band of sympathizers, fearlessly performing a last act of friendship by walking with them to their place of execution. There were Sir George Blagge and Nicholas Throckmorton with his two brothers, George and Kenelm, and a certain John Louthe. Such open support for the heretics was tantamount to a defiance of the authorities which had condemned them. Someone in the crowd shouted out to warn the courtiers of the danger they were in, "Ye are all marked that come to them. Take heed to your lives." But the gentlemen stayed with the prisoners until the last possible moment. John Louthe even went so far as to shout out to the councillors, "I ask vengeance on you all that do thus burn a member of Christ!" He was lucky to escape with no more than a blow from an angry neighbour.[128]

What was remarkable about such a demonstration of support for the prisoners was not so much the courage of the demonstrators, as the fact that they got away with it. That suggests that the councillors thought it wiser to tolerate their behaviour than to order their arrest. To send troops into an emotionally charged crowd, divided into rival camps might well have spelled disaster. Instead, they pressed on with the obligatory ritual demanded by the occasion.

---

127   Foxe named this third man as Nicholas Bellanian, a Shropshire priest, but this seems to be an error. See *Acts and Monuments*, Volume V, pp. 550–51.

128   Strype J. *Narratives of the Days of the Reformation*, 1859, pp. 44–45.

The condemned were bound to their stakes. Anne's legs would not hold her and she could only be kept upright by a strong chain passed round her waist. There was to be no question even now of a speedy end. The whole prolonged ritual had to be enacted. First of all the sermon. Poor Nicholas Shaxton had been singled out for the honour of preaching to the four heretics whose souls were in such imminent danger. This was the last act in his public humiliation. But the unfortunate man could hardly make himself heard. As well as the continuous bustle and murmur of the crowd he had the unquenchable Anne Askew to contend with. She paid close attention to every word of Shaxton's address and gave a running commentary on it, pointing out all the learned doctor's errors.

At last the ex-bishop was done preaching and thankfully clambered down from the pulpit. The next formality to be observed was the final offer of pardon in return for a recantation. Wriothesley sent down a message but the condemned refused even to read it. Anne spoke for her companions when she called out, "I came not hither to deny my Lord and Master."

During the sermon, men had been piling faggots around the stakes and all was now ready for the execution. John Russell as an act of mercy had ordered bags of gunpowder to be hung round the bodies of the four heretics. When the other councillors saw this being done they became alarmed and Russell had to assure them that the bags had been most carefully filled and placed. There was no fear of a violent explosion. The moment had now arrived. The executioner stood ready with a flaming torch. The crowd fell silent and Sir Martin Bowes's simple command was clearly heard across Smithfield. "*Fiat Justitia!*" And so, in Foxe's words:

> They thus confirming one another with mutual
> exhortations tarried looking for the tormentor and the fire,
> which at the last flaming round about them, consumed
> their blessed bodies in happy martyrdom, in the year of
> our salvation 1546.[129]

---

129   Foxe J. *Acts and Monuments*, Volume V, p. 551.

Anne Askew and her companions were the last victims of the Act of Six Articles to suffer death in London and almost the last of the thirty-one victims to perish anywhere as a result of that legislation.

PART 3

After

CHAPTER 11

Catherine and Anne in
Historical Perspective

It was not so long ago that you burned Anne Askew
for a piece of bread, yet came yourselves to believe the
doctrine for which you burned her.[130]

*I*n 1550 Joan Bocher, an anti-trinitarian Anabaptist, threw that
taunt at Thomas Cranmer during her heresy trial.[131] It must have
stung the archbishop because there was more than a little truth in
the allegation. During the last years of Henry's reign he had been
struggling with the traditional doctrine of the mass. If Christ's
words "This is my body … This is my blood" were not to be taken
as indicating a corporeal presence in the elements, how should
they be understood? It was in discussion with his friend Nicholas
Ridley (who was appointed Bishop of Rochester in 1547) that
he eventually arrived at a formula close to, if not identical with,
Zwinglianism:

… although Christ in his human nature, substantially,
really, corporally, naturally, and sensibly be present with

---

130   Strype J. *Memorials of Archbishop Cranmer*, Volume II, i, p. 335.
131   Though Robert Parsons, the Catholic protagonist, writing early in
the next century claimed that Joan was a member of Anne's "sect", there
is no evidence for any close connection and Joan's theology was more
extreme than Anne's.

his Father in heaven, yet sacramentally and spiritually he is here present. For in water, bread, and wine he is present as in signs and sacraments.[132]

Cranmer's theology was more sophisticated and subtle than Anne Askew's, but the distinction may not have been clear to most ordinary worshippers who attended their parish churches to experience the new "Protestant" services which came into being in 1549. The old Latin mass was replaced by an English "Lord's Supper or Holy Communion". The elements were given to the communicants in both kinds with the words: "Eat this in remembrance that Christ died for thee ... drink this in remembrance that Christ's blood was shed for thee ..." The impact of the changes was enormous, but the new liturgy had not reached its final form. It was contained in two prayer books (1549 and 1552) which moved by stages further and further from the medieval rite. Even so, these innovations did not satisfy all leaders of what had become the official English church and more adjustments were under consideration when the death of Edward VI ushered in the reign of Catholic Mary Tudor and the reintroduction of the Latin mass.

But we must backtrack to the immediate aftermath of the gruesome events of July 1546 if we are to assess the contributions of the queen and the heretic to England's Reformation. The immediate reaction of many evangelicals in the capital was to flee. Scores left the country, while others remained but with distance between themselves and the heresy hunters. This failed to save some of them, as a report from the Council of the North in December indicates:

At one of the sessions of the Six Articles by us held within your Majesty's city of York, were convicted two persons, sacramentaries, the one named Richard Burdone and the other John Grove, who repaired hither immediately after the execution of Anne Ayscough, Lascelles and others, and were present at the same. And we have spared for a time the execution of the said Burdone and Grove, until

---

132   Cox J. E. (ed.) *Works of Thomas Cranmer*, Cambridge, 1844–6, Volume I, p. 47.

your Majesty's pleasure be further known therein, upon
consideration that neither of them do keep nor stand
in any such opinions, but recant and sore lament their
offences, referring themselves wholly to the mercy of
God and Your majesty's further pleasure, whereof we
most humbly beseech Your Highness that we may have
knowledge ...[133]

The Smithfield burnings doubtless had the effect desired by the
authorities – in the short term. There must have been several radicals
in various locales who avoided detection by flight or quickly buckled
under interrogation. But, by the autumn, the heat was off. There
are only records of three burnings (in East Anglia) between August
and November. Soon after the execution of Anne and her fellow
sufferers, a London citizen, John Warne, was condemned to a similar
fate, but direct appeals to Henry by friends at court secured his release
and that of two Suffolk radicals also earmarked for execution.

The easing of pressure was in large measure the result of
political changes at the top. With Seymour and Dudley back
in regular attendance at the Council and the king increasingly
confined to his own quarters, the evangelicals were able to assert
more influence. Sir Anthony Denny, a strong advocate of reform,
as chief gentleman of the Privy Chamber monitored access to the
king but, more than that, he was in a position of power by virtue
of his custody of the royal dry stamp. This was an image of the
king's signature which was pressed onto documents and then inked
in. It was entrusted to Denny in order to relieve Henry of dealing
personally with large amounts of paperwork.

With evangelicals well placed in the households of the king,
the queen, and the prince, the conservatives needed to assert their
supremacy in the Council. This made for a tense atmosphere
around the table and one that emanated outwards to the parties
they represented in the country as a whole. In a report of 10
November the French ambassador de Selve commented:

---

133 *State Papers, published under the authority of His Majesty's Commission*,
1836, V, p. 577.

> Here is a great bruit of dissension and "mutations de état" [political instability] among the principal men of this realm; and the day before yesterday command was given to the mayor of this town and to the justices of the peace in the provinces to enquire secretly for such as talked treason against the king or knew of any talk or conspiracy against him.[134]

According to one account, an argument in the Council ended with Dudley slapping Gardiner's face. Whether or not that rumour was unfounded, it does support the impression of serious conflict.

Much of that conflict had to do with the rivalry of the Howards and the Seymours. The Duke of Norfolk and his son, the Earl of Surrey, hated the upstart family who claimed semi-royal status by virtue of their relationship with the house of Tudor. Edward Seymour, Earl of Hertford, was an arrogant *arriviste* whose standing with his brother-in-law Henry VIII was bolstered by his military successes. The Howards, as holders of the most ancient and prestigious noble title, could not tolerate his presumption. Norfolk was a sufficient realist to realize that conflict was unproductive. As we have seen, he attempted to forge a marriage alliance with his rival. This was undermined by the headstrong Surrey, who advanced counter-claims to affinity with the Crown and went so far as to emblazon on his own escutcheon not only the royal coat of arms but also that of Edward the Confessor, thus claiming more ancient royal lineage than the Tudors. There seems little doubt that this was the dissension referred to by ambassador de Selve.

Surrey set in train a chain of events that proved fatal to him when he got into an argument with Sir George Blagge over his heraldic pretension. The earl sent a truculent letter to his erstwhile friend, who, though a mere knight, was presuming to challenge his betters. Blagge passed the letter to Seymour, who was only too happy to discomfort his rivals by showing the letter to the king on 1 December. From that point the matter followed the conventional course: Surrey was arrested and his enemies were permitted to carry

---

134   *L & P*, XXI, pt. ii, p. 381.

out a full investigation. Among those who now testified against the earl was Richard Southwell, who, like Blagge, had transferred political and religious allegiance to the Seymour camp. Pigeons were coming home to roost. By 12 December, not only Surrey, but also his father, were in the Tower. A month later, the earl was tried and found guilty, and on 19 January he was beheaded. A few days later Norfolk was declared guilty by association and an Act of Attainder condemned him to death.

At the same time, Stephen Gardiner also forfeited the king's support. Henry had required an exchange of Crown lands with others belonging to the Diocese of Winchester. The bishop was foolish enough to demur. Henry was furious. Gardiner, realizing his folly too late, tried to gain access to the king, but was unsuccessful. On 2 December, he was obliged to put in writing his grovelling apology. He lamented his "want of circumspection" and continued, "I on my knees desire pardon … I would gladly supply my want could I have such help from you as others have had".[135] We scarcely need to read between the lines to sense Gardiner's resentment that his conciliar rivals enjoyed that direct contact with the king that he was now denied. This deliberate distancing was Henry's well-established way of marking a servant's (occasionally fatal) fall from grace. Sometimes time healed the breach and the royal anger subsided. Not on this occasion. On 26 December, Henry sent for his will and made changes to his testamentary depositions. He ordered Gardiner's name to be removed from the list of councillors named as regents during the minority of his successor. The bishop, he said, was "a wilful man, not meet to be about his son".

Thus was the way prepared for the reformist government which assumed power on the death of Henry VIII on 28 January 1547. England now was delivered – or fell – into the hands of an evangelical establishment.

> Determined to join the religious revolution in the rest
> of Europe: to destroy the old world of devotion of
> the English Church, which as a result of the political

---

135 *L & P*, XXI, pt. ii, 487.

seesaw of Henry's thirty-eighth year, now lay helpless
before them, a severed limb of the Western Latin
church. Edward's leading political advisers were poised to
implement the alternative programme for religion which
evangelicalism promised.[136]

The kingdom of Edward VI was set upon a self-concious
idealogical course of change. Henry's Reformation, though
momentous, had never been a predominantly religious movement.
The old king who made provision in his will for masses to be
said for his soul in perpetuity cannot, under any stretch of the
imagination, be called "Protestant". His interest had always been
the establishment and maintenance of royal supremacy in church
and state. It was Cromwell and Cranmer, assisted by a growing
army of preachers and writers, who had begun to build on the
bedrock of the indomitable royal will a new, independent nation
church with a cornerstone of freely available vernacular Scripture
and buttressed by the doctrine of justification by only faith. It is
impossible to avoid the cliché of describing Edward VI's brief
reign as a turning point in English history.

But that is not the story being told in this book. What I have
tried to explore is the build-up to this monumental change. It is
story replete with the actions of brave, visionary men and women.
Between 1547 and 1552 it was easy for evangelicals to proceed
"full steam ahead" with the work of reconstruction – tearing down
the remaining "idolatrous" images, reshaping public worship,
proclaiming Gospel-based social reform. Those who preceded
them in the religiously ambivalent reign of Henry VIII had a much
more difficult and convoluted path to walk in discovering and
remaining true to their biblical faith. In focusing attention on two
remarkable women I have tried to describe how the Reformation
caught on within the educated classes of early Tudor England.
Uniquely we can see into the minds of Anne Askew and Catherine
Parr because they published under their own names their beliefs
and experiences (and were the first English women to do so).

---

136   MacCulloch D. *Tudor Church Militant*, London, 2000, p. 8.

Because they wrote we can discern what they believed and also what impact they had through their books. The first part of that story has been told. It only remains to assess the impact of Anne Askew and Catherine Parr in the aftermath of July 1546.

The queen survived the heretic by less than twenty-six months – months marked by alternating joy and misery. The death of Henry VIII in January 1547 allowed her, at last, to follow her heart in deciding on her fourth marriage. Less than two weeks later she wrote to Thomas Seymour, brother of Edward Seymour, now Duke of Somerset and Protector of the Realm,

> My Lord,
>
> I send you my most humble and hearty commendations, being desirous to know how ye have done since I saw you. I pray you be not offended with me in that I send sooner to you than I said I would. For my promise was but once in a fortnight … I would not have you to think that this mine honest goodwill towards you to proceed of any sudden motion or passion. For, as truly as God is God, my mind was fully bent the other time I was at liberty, to marry you before any man I knew. Howbeit, God withstood my will therein most vehemently for a time and, through His grace and goodness, made that possible which seemeth to me most unpossible – that was, made me to renounce utterly mine own will, and to follow His will most willingly. It were too long to write all the process of this matter. If I live, I shall declare it to you myself. I can say nothing but, as my lady of Suffolk saith, "God is a marvellous man."
>
> By her that is yours to serve and obey during her life,
>
> Katherine the Queen KP[137]

---

137   Mueller 2011, pp. 130–31.

Clearly, Catherine and Thomas had been in intimate contact by the time the widow wrote this letter. She threw herself with ardour into the revival of her old love. Her passion is readily understandable. She was thirty-five and had dutifully bestowed her best years on the care of older husbands. Now she grasped with both hands the prospect of a love match and the possibility of bearing children. Thomas Seymour, now Lord Admiral, was only four years her senior, still handsome and dashing. And ambitious. He saw himself as a rival to his brother and was determined to use marriage as a power lever in his own political schemes. According to gossip, on the death of the old king he was quick to weigh up the advantages of taking to wife Anne of Cleves, Princess Mary, or Princess Elizabeth. But Catherine was either oblivious of this or chose not to believe it. Her relationship with Thomas in those early months of 1547 has the flavour of teenage romance, marked by written avowals of love and clandestine meetings. Sometime in May the couple were married.

From the repercussions of this we see the dowager queen in a new light. As the new regime established itself, the men and women at the centre of national life jostled to assert themselves and claim those positions they assumed to be theirs by right. Neither the ex-queen nor Edward's younger uncle were allotted places on the regency council. They both resented this. In addition there began a competition for precedence between Catherine and Anne, Duchess of Somerset, the Protector's wife, who was not prepared to play second fiddle to the wife of her husband's younger brother. When the news of the marriage (contracted without the permission of the king or the duke) came out, Anne was not slow to voice her anger. Catherine responded with equal malice, as she told her husband:

> ... my lord your brother hath this afternoon a little made me warm. It was fortunate we were so much distant, for I suppose else I should have bitten him. What cause have they to fear [you] having such a wife? It is requisite for them continually to pray for a short despatch of that hell [that is, they should pray to be delivered from their anger

and jealousy]. Tomorrow, or else upon Saturday … I will
see the King, where I intend to utter all my choler to my
lord, your brother …[138]

Catherine's life changed drastically – and not in all ways for
the better. She now spent most of her time either at her
manor in Chelsea or at her husband's home, Sudeley Castle in
Gloucestershire. The old camaraderie of the queen's chamber
was a thing of the past. Her close relations with her step-
children now took second place to supporting Thomas in the
Seymour power struggle. Princess Mary soon moved to take up
residence on her Norfolk estate. Catherine's correspondence
with the young king remained warm in tone but was coloured
by Thomas's attempts to buy Edward's affection and turn him
against the Protector. Elizabeth did spend several months in the
Lord Admiral's household but that arrangement ended in tears
because Thomas became over-friendly with the Tudor princess.
In June 1548, Catherine complained that her husband's behaviour
with the teenager was inappropriate and sent her away.

By this time Catherine was pregnant and looking forward to
a real family life of her own. Elizabeth's place had been taken by
Thomas's ward, the devout and intelligent Lady Jane Grey, who,
as a granddaughter of Henry VIII's sister Mary, had her place in
the Tudor succession. This was yet another element in the Lord
Admiral's strategy of gaining proximity to the Crown, but his wife
enjoyed having another well-educated evangelical enthusiast as
her protégée. On 30 August, Catherine was safely delivered of a
daughter. Unfortunately, she fell prey to one of the scourges of
the age, puerperal fever. Her few remaining days were rendered
wretched, not only by her illness, but also because of her suspicion
that her husband was poisoning her. Whether this was the result
of her delirium or whether she had come to realize that Thomas's
ambition was stronger than his love had ever been we cannot
know. Certainly, the Lord Admiral stepped up his campaign to
supplant his brother as soon as his wife had died, an event that

138   Mueller 2011, pp. 140–41.

occurred in the early hours of 5 September 1548. Her obsequies were conducted in English. There were no prayers for the dead. The evangelical sermon was preached by Miles Coverdale. It was the first Protestant funeral of a royal personage in England.

Scarcely six months later Catherine's husband followed her to the grave. His headstrong, headlong rush into action against his brother was certainly too haphazard to be called rebellion but Parliament had no difficulty judging it to be treason. Seymour was attainted and, on 20 March 1549, was executed on Tower Hill.

Out in the shires life was less dramatic. Francis Askew showed himself to be an acquisitive and successful empire builder. In the early years of Queen Elizabeth's reign he concentrated on making himself the richest gentleman in the county. He had for some years had his eyes on a large area of crown land and administration known as the Soke of Caistor. It comprised "The Manor of Caistor, etc. and ten messuages, two hundred acres of land, one hundred acres of meadow, one hundred acres of pasture and forty shillings rent in Caistor, Gresby, Houghton, Fulnetby, North Kelsey, and Ancholme".[139] Despite sustained efforts, Francis was unsuccessful in his suit for this land when the queen disposed of it in 1557. Instead it went to the courtier Sir Thomas Hastings. Weeks of hard bargaining followed. Hastings was quite prepared to sell his new acquisition, but there were other suitors, namely Sir William Cardell and Lady Elizabeth Dalyson. On 14 October 1557, a deal was made; the Soke was granted jointly to the three suitors but was to revert eventually to the heirs of Elizabeth Dalyson. Francis Askew accepted this arrangement but his ambition refused to be contained by it. On 15 December, he bought out Sir William Cardell. Thus matters remained for two years. Then fortune played into Sir Francis's hands. On the same day, 10 October 1559, Francis's wife and Lady Dalyson's husband died. After a decent delay the head of the Askew family married widow Dalyson and thus brought into the family not only the property inherited by Elizabeth from her late husband, but also the Soke of Caistor. By

---

139   Brewster H. C. *South Kelsey Notes*, MS in Lincoln Cathedral Library, 1898, p. 67.

such manoeuvres Sir Francis Askew prospered and was able to leave to his eldest son estates valued (in the opinion of the family chronicler) at over £20,000.

Francis died in 1564, a convinced Protestant. This is clearly shown by the wording of his will. Does it also suggest a still lingering remorse over the betrayal of his sister?

> I bequeath my soul to Almighty God, by whose merits and passion I trust only to be saved and through no good deeds of my own but with the publican I do confess myself to be a sinner and do appeal to God's mercy and not to his justice, knowing him to be a merciful Lord in whom I only trust.[140]

Perhaps Francis's greatest dynastic achievement was the marriage of his son, William, into the nobility. The girl in question was Anne, daughter of Edward Fiennes Clinton, Earl of Lincoln. Alas for Sir Francis Askew's ambition. The family chronicler records the subsequent history of this marriage and does not fail to draw a moral:

> … For the sequel, this much I have since observed, that his [i.e. Francis's] son and heir in few years wasted the better part of his patrimony (not to be redeemed at this day with twenty thousand pounds) by yielding over much to the unbridled vanities of another Anne Askew, his wife. Thus it pleased the Lord in his wisdom to give honour to our family through such a person as the world then held reproachful [i.e. Anne Askew the martyr], and contrariwise to impair the state and reputation of the same, by such a match as, in the judgement of man (for she was honourably descended) should rather have given more estimation unto it.[141]

---

140 Principal Probate Registry, Morison, I.

141 Ayscough E. *A Historie containing the Warres Treaties Marriages and other occurents between England and Scotland, from King William the Conqueror until the happy Union of them both in our gracious King James*, 1607, pp. 306–7.

We might add that not only did Anne Clinton waste much of the carefully garnered Askew wealth but she also failed to do what convention expected of her – provide her provide her husband with an heir.

By this time England was, of course, securely within the Protestant fold. The theological issues which had convulsed the nation in the middle years of the sixteenth century and which had shaped the destinies of the queen and the heretic were long gone. Or were they? The *media via* espoused by Elizabeth I did not satisfy all her people. Catholics took the place of the earlier radicals as covert worshippers who met in secret and went in fear of the knock on the door in the middle of the night. At the other end of the confessional spectrum there were Anglican Puritans and separatists for whom the Reformation had not gone far enough. Some areas of the country were notorious for their resistance of the Elizabethan settlement. None more so than the home turf of several of the families we have been considering. The whole area of Lincolnshire and Nottinghamshire around Retford, Worksop, Gainsborough, and Newark was a Puritan stronghold until well into the seventeenth century, where it became the breeding ground of the Pilgrim Fathers.

Where, then, do our female authors fit into the wider story of the English Reformation? Catherine Parr's reputation tends to suffer because she is only thought of by many as being one of the "Six Wives". She was the one who "survived" and her story has little of the high drama that marked the careers of her predecessors. The popular perception of her seems to be as a combination of nursemaid and bluestocking. It comes as something of a surprise to learn that at the time of her marriage to King Henry she was only about thirty. Certainly she was mature for her years. That maturity had been gained from her upbringing at court, her experience with her former husbands, her involvement in the upheaval of 1536–37, and her study of the theological concerns that were underlying the traumatic changes disturbing Europe during her early years. Among Henry's wives only Anne Boleyn was as involved as Catherine in the ferment of ideas and, like Anne, she had come down on the side of reform.

What makes Catherine Parr stand out, not only from Henry's other wives but also from all other English women of her age, is her writings. Her intense spirituality and her struggle to acquire a strong personal faith are accessible to us because she believed it important to take the quite unprecedented step of publishing her own meditations on Scripture and her own spiritual history.

The Lamentation of a Sinner is a personal testimony of the type we normally associate with evangelicals of the post-Bunyan era. It is an account of the author's conversion from a merely formal (what she calls "historical") faith to a personal response to the love of God and the receiving of assurance. Like innumerable Christians who have experienced a dramatic conversion, Catherine felt the need to tell the world about it. Publication was part of the mission to which she believed herself called. We can believe her when she says that it was obedience to God that made her accept Henry's proposal, and not the allure of wealth and status.

The Lamentation of a Sinner was published on 5 November 1547 and carried a preface by William Cecil, a close associate of Protector Somerset, who became his secretary a few months later. He extolled Catherine's virtues and urged the reader, "See and learn hereby what she hath done: then mayst thou practise and amend that thou canst".[142] The book thus had the endorsement of the regime. Whether that enthusiastic support survived Catherine's marriage to Thomas Seymour and the bitter family feuding to which she became a party is doubtful. Certainly, this spiritual autobiography had a shorter shelf life than her earlier devotional writings. *Prayers or Meditations* went through thirteen editions in the sixteenth century. However, the *Lamentation* remained popular, particularly with dissenters during the Civil War period. Its candour and emotionalism certainly chimed with seventeenth-century pietism and Wesleyan religious introspection. It provided a classic conversion narrative for use by preachers and evangelists, who could point out that even queens had climbed the ladder of repentance and faith. Today, Catherine's introspection and her compulsion to break into the male presence of book production

---

142   Mueller 2011, p. 445.

in order to spread the truths she had learned have won her name admirers among feminist historians. Paradoxically, the queen would not have recognized herself as striking a blow for women's equality. Though Catherine was the first English woman to publish under her own name, she was just one example of a phenomenon that had appeared in Europe over the previous two decades.

> If God has given grace to some good women, revealing
> to them by his holy scriptures something holy and good,
> should they hesitate to write … it would be foolish to hide
> the talent that God has given us.[143]

So wrote the ex-prioress turned ardent Calvinist, Marie Dentière, in 1536, yet even she published her defence of the Genevan reform model anonymously. Marie was representative of a small but significant band of female writers who offered the public devotional works and trenchant doctrinal tracts. They all faced the problems, intrinsic to Bible students of all epochs, of working out exactly what the word of God *does* say about women. The New Testament clearly taught that the economy of salvation embraced equally all believers, irrespective of sex [Galatians 3:28] but it also made clear that wives were subservient to their husbands and had no teaching role in the church [1 Timothy 2:12]. This issue reared its head, as we have seen, in the tribulations of both the queen and the heretic. There is a certain doctrinal irony about the way each responded to the challenge. Catherine, the moderate reformer and dutiful wife, broke the taboo against female authorship. Anne the radical, who left her husband and defied convention by her gospelling, did not deliberately venture into print.

Posterity owes the first-hand accounts of Anne Askew's trials to John Bale (1495–1563). This ex-Carmelite friar abandoned his religious vocation in the 1530s and devoted himself to writing plays and prose works. His talents were recognized by Thomas Cromwell, who used Bale in his anti-papal propaganda. He was a voluminous writer; a scholar with the popular touch. He made

---

143   Stjerna K. *Women and the Reformation*, Oxford, 2009, p. 135.

many enemies by his vigorous and "earthy" denunciations of Catholic life and practice. After Cromwell's fall, Bale considered it wise to seek refuge abroad. He was in the Lutheran state of Hesse in 1546 and it was there that Anne Askew's autobiographical writings reached him only months after her execution. They had been smuggled out of England by Dutch merchants.

The whole style of the written material changed drastically in Bale's hands. Anne's accounts of her two 1546 interrogations were designed for her fellow believers in London and the writer's main concern was to scotch the story being spread by the authorities that she had signed a formal recantation. By the time this material reached Bale, Anne was a celebrity in evangelical circles and her martyrdom was headline news. The editor saw the opportunity to fit this sensational story into his wider agenda. This was to vilify what the 1549 Book of Common Prayer would describe as "the tyranny of the Bishop of Rome and all his detestable enormities". He was concerned to show that the reformed communities were the true church and that their enemies were agents of the Antichrist. Bale trawled the Bible and church history to find comparisons with those in his own day who suffered for righteousness' sake. What he did with Anne's story was to break it up into several chunks, interspersed with his own acerbic comments. One passage is sufficient to indicate both his subject matter and his style. The sufferings of Anne and her colleagues, he explained, were similar to those of Christ:

> Pilate shewed the accused all favour possible. He examined him privately, he gave him friendly words, he bade him not fear to speak. He heard him with gentleness, he counselled with him that he might the more freely suppress their mad fury, and he promised, they [the Jewish priests] should do him no wrong in case he would utter his full mind, John 18. Far contrary to this were Wriothesley and Rich, which not all ignorant of the bishop's beastly errors, maliciously without all fear of God and shame of the world, executed upon this godly woman most terrible tyranny. Pilate spake for the innocent,

189

excused him, defended him, laid forth the law, pleaded to him sharply, required them to shew mercy, alleged for him their custom, declared him an innocent and sought by all means to deliver him, Matthew 27. These perjured magistrates Wriothesley and Rich, not only examined this innocent woman with rigour, but also hated her, scorned her, reviled her, condemned her for an heretic and with unspeakable torments sought to enforce her to bring by accusation other noble women and men to death.[144]

Bale wasted no time in publishing Anne's dramatic story. It appeared in two parts: *The First Examination of Anne Askew, lately martyred in Smithfield* was printed at Wesel in the Lower Rhineland and was on sale in England by the year's end. *The Later Examination* followed within weeks. From a commercial point of view the timing could not have been better. When Henry VIII died on 28 January 1547, the campaign against heretical literature also died. Readers could now openly buy these accounts of the sensational Askew trials about which rumours had been circulating for months. And so they did. When the Wesel editions were exhausted, the two books were combined and went through four English printings before 1553. They spawned other publications. One was *A Ballard of Anne Askew*, a song supposedly written by the condemned woman in Newgate Prison. During the reign of Mary Tudor (1553–58) the Protestant scholar John Foxe fled to Basel where he became a printer's proofreader alongside his friend and fellow exile, John Bale. Foxe was working on his monumental *Acts and Monuments of the Christian Religion*, a collection of stories of men and women who, from the earliest days, had promoted and suffered for the "true" faith. The work went through four editions, growing in size with each issue, but Anne's story had its place there from the very first (Latin) version of 1559. Foxe incorporated Bale's material, shorn of the editor's trenchant commentary. The Lincolnshire gentlewoman thus took her place in the galaxy of those who had

---

144   Beilin E. V. (ed.) *The Examinations of Anne Askew*, Oxford, 1996, pp. 151–52.

borne witness to Christian truth ever since the persecution of Nero. For generations, Foxe's *Book of Martyrs* was second only to the Bible as the best-selling English text. Anne's story entered our literary bloodstream and has remained there.

If that were not sufficient evidence of the significance of the Askew narrative, we can look for more to the reactions of the traditionalists. As early as May 1547 Bishop Gardiner was protesting to the Duke of Somerset about Bale's books. They were, he claimed, "very pernicious, seditious and slanderous" and they had distorted the facts about Anne's interrogations. He deplored the encouragement given to women to read and interpret Scripture for themselves and raised the spectre of social chaos should such ideas catch on.[145] It hardly needs saying that the bishop would not have denounced the accounts of Anne's persecution if they had not already become dangerously popular. Once again we find ourselves faced with the gender issue. Gardiner genuinely believed that free access to the word of God by women, on equal terms with men, was a weevil which would eat away at the fabric of society. This remained a favourite objection of conservatives to free access to the Bible. A hundred years later when England was plagued by sectarian conflict, the popular satirist John Taylor wrote:

When women preach and cobblers pray,
The fiends in hell make holiday.[146]

We tend to associate the English Reformation either with Henry's conflict with the papacy or with debates over "faith", "grace", "penance", "free will", "church", "divine sovereignty", and other profound theological issues. But it was the availability of the Bible in English that threw a bomb into English society. Its explosion reverberated down the centuries, changing millions of lives in a myriad different ways. We are familiar with the stories of people who responded to the challenge of holy writ to become missionaries, social reformers, philanthropists, as well as preachers

---

145   Muller J. (ed.) *The Letters of Stephen Gardiner*, Cambridge, 1933, pp. 276ff.

146   J. Taylor, *Lucifer's Lackey*, 1640.

and evangelists. But the examples are legion of Christians who have and still do impact on the lives of their contemporaries and later generations. In the 1540s two very different women wrestled with the word of God and what it was saying to them. They reached conclusions that did not, at all points, agree. Yet both were committed to reaching others with divine truth.

Mary Lascelles, a collateral descendant of John Lascelles who perished by fire in the flames of Smithfield, died in 1615. Her memorial brass in Worksop parish church reads:

Her holy and religious care
To have the Gospel taught,
Did always argue public good
Before her own she sought.

That would serve equally well as an epitaph for Catherine Parr, queen of England, and Anne Askew, the Lincolnshire gospeller.

Bibliography

Ayscough, E. *A Historie containing the Warres Treaties Marriages and other occurents between England and Scotland, from King William the Conqueror until the happy Union of them both in our gracious King James*, 1607.

Bailey S. "Robert Wisdom under Persecution, 1541–1543", *Journal of Ecclesiastical History*, II:ii, 2011.

Bale J. *Select Works* (ed. H. Christmas), Cambridge, 1849.

Barzun J. *From Dawn to Decadence*, New York, 2000.

Beilin E. V. (ed.) *The Examinations of Anne Askew*, Oxford, 1996.

Brewster H. C. *South Kelsey Notes*, MS in Lincoln Cathedral Library, 1898.

Brigden S. *London and the Reformation*, Oxford, 1989.

Clay J. W. (ed.) *North Country Wills*, I, Publications of the Surtees Society, Volume cxvi.

Cox J. E. (ed.) *Works of Thomas Cranmer*, Cambridge, 1844–6.

Dasent J. R. (ed.) *Acts of the Privy Council of England Volume 1, 1542–1547*, London, 1890, British History Online, http://www.british-history.ac.uk/acts-privy-council/vol1.

Davies M. B. (trans.) Extracts from the Welsh chronicle of Elis Gruffydd, in *Bulletin of the Faculty of Arts*, 11/1, Cairo, 1949.

Dickens A. G. *Lollards and Protestant in the Diocese of York 1509–1558*, Hull, 1959.

Elton G. R. *Policy and Police – The Enforcement of the Reformation in the Age of Thomas Cromwell*, Cambridge, 1972.

Foxe J. *Acts and Monuments of John Foxe*, ed. S.R. Cattley, 1841.

Gairdner J. (ed.) *Letters and Papers, Foreign and Domestic, Henry VIII*, London, 1888, British History Online, http://www.british-history.ac.uk/letters-papers-hen8.

Grey Friars' Chronicle, Camden Society, Old Series, 1852.

Gunther K. *Reformation Unbound – Protestant Vision of Reform in England, 1525–1590*, Cambridge, 2014.

Historical Manuscripts Commission, *The Manuscripts of Shrewsbury and Coventry Corporations [Etc] Fourth Report, Appendix: Part X*, London, 1899, British History Online, http://www.british-history.ac.uk/hist-mss-comm/vol47/pt10

Krahn C. *Dutch Anabaptism: Origin, Spread, Life and Thought (1450–1600)*, The Hague, 1968.

Lambert M. *Medieval Heresy – Popular Movements from the Gregorian Reform to the Reformation*, Oxford, 1992.

MacCulloch D. *Thomas Cranmer: A Life*, London, 1996.

MacCulloch D. *Tudor Church Militant*, London, 2000.

Mueller J. (ed.) *Katherine Parr – Complete Works and Correspondence*, Chicago, 2011.

Muller J. (ed.) *The Letters of Stephen Gardiner*, Cambridge, 1933.

Rabil A. (ed.) *Henricus Cornelius Agrippa – Declaration on the Nobility and Pre-eminence of the Female Sex*, Chicago, 1996.

Redworth G. *In Defence of the Church Catholic: The Life of Stephen Gardiner*, Oxford, 1990.

Robinson H. (ed.) *Original Letters Relative to the English Reformation*, Cambridge, 1846.

Rupp G. *The Righteousness of God*, New York, 1953.

Ryrie A. *The Gospel and Henry VIII*, Cambridge, 2003.

Stjerna K. *Women and the Reformation*, Oxford, 2009.

Stow J. *Annals of the Reformation*, 1601.

Strype J. *Ecclesiastical Memorials of the Church of England*, 1823.

Strype J. *Memorials of the Most Reverend Father in God, Thomas Cranmer*, Oxford, 1848-54.

Strype J. *Narratives of the Days of the Reformation*, Volume 77, Cambridge, 1859.

Thompson C. (trans.) *Collected Works of Erasmus – Colloquies*, Toronto/Buffalo/London, 1997.

Walter H. (ed.) *An Answer to Sir Thomas More's Dialogue*, Cambridge, 1850.

Wriothesley C. A. *Chronicle of England*, Camden Society, Second Series, 1875.

Index

Index terms within footnotes are indicated by an "n" followed by the footnote number.

Act for the Advancement of True Religion (1543) 57, 72, 84, 99

Act of Six Articles (1539): Anne Askew 84, 91, 110, 171; doctrine of English church 57; heresy persecutions 57–9, 78, 91, 124, 131, 140, 176; modification 87–8

Act of Supremacy (1534) 20, 21, 52

Acts and Monuments of the Christian Religion (Foxe) 111n68, 144n103, 168, 169n127, 170, 190

The Address to the Christian Nobility of the German Nation (Luther) 15

adult baptism 61

Anabaptism: Anne Askew 109–10, 112, 168; Catherine Parr 138, 155; Henry VIII on 55; Joan Bocher trial 175; martyrdom 105; memorialism 110; rise of 61, 62, 89

Anne Boleyn, Queen *see* Boleyn, Anne

Anne of Cleves 54–5, 57, 60, 182

Answer to More (Tyndale) 42

Articles Devised by the King's Highness's Majesty to Establish Christian Quietness and Unity Among Us (1536) 56–7

Ascham, Roger 146

Aske, Robert 25, 26, 27

Askew, Anne: arrests 90–2, 110–14, 133–5; Bale writings 147n105, 188–90; Bible on women 188; birth of 13; and Bonner 114–20, 133; and Catherine Parr 88–9, 144, 148, 151; confession 119–20; conversion 34–5, 43; Council questioning 136–40; death of 141–2, 154, 160n119, 168–71, 176–7; divorce appeal 82–4, 91; education 35; on eucharist 90, 109–10; female authorship 188; final acts 105–6; Foxe writings 190–1; and Francis Askew 63, 83, 133–5, 166; in historical perspective 123, 175, 180, 181, 192; imprisonment in Compter 114–20; imprisonment in Newgate 163–8; inquisition and sentence 141–3; interrogation in Tower 154–60; last written words 166–8; marriage to Thomas Kyme 43–4, 52–3, 63, 133; moves to London 84–6, 88–9; New Learning 38; personality 90; racking of 158–9, 164, 165, 168; radicalism 62–3; Reformation origins 38–9; "ruffling" aftermath 33; upbringing 9, 16; writings 110–11, 147n105, 180–1, 188–91

Askew, Anne (née Clinton) 185–6

Askew,   (brother of Anne) 13, 16, 19, 20, 24, 31, 84

Askew, Edward (brother of Anne) 13, 16, 19, 24, 84

Askew, Elizabeth (mother of Anne) 12, 13

Askew, Elizabeth (née Hansard) (wife of Francis) 13–14, 16, 184

Askew, Sir Francis (brother of Anne): Anne Askew divorce appeal 63, 83; Anne Askew persecution 133–5, 166; at Cambridge University 14, 17, 18, 19; and Cranmer 19; death of 185; Lincolnshire Rebellion 24; Soke of Caistor land 184–5; upbringing 13, 14, 16; war with France 84

Askew, Jane (sister of Anne) 16

Askew, John 11

Askew, Martha (sister of Anne) 13, 16, 43

Askew, Sir William (1422–56) 11

Askew, William, of Stallingborough (d.1509) 11–12

Askew, Sir William (1486–1540) (father of Anne): Bawmborough hearings 44–6; death of 52; evangelical "heresy" 17; family life 12–13, 16, 17, 18–20; and Hansard estates 13–14; in Henry VIII court 12–13; knighthood 13; Lincolnshire Rebellion 23–5, 31; marriages 12, 14; at South Kelsey Hall 9, 14, 17, 18–20; and Tyrrwhit 45–6, 52

Askew, William (son of Francis Askew) 185–6

Augsburg Confession (1530) 106

Ayscough, Bishop William (1395–1450) 11

Ayscough, Sir Edward (nephew of Anne Askew) 133, 134

Ayscough, Sir William see Askew, Sir William (father of Anne)

Babington, Sir Anthony 50

Babington, John 49, 50

The Babylonian Captivity of the Church (Luther) 15

Baker, Sir John 155

Bale, John 41, 110n68, 113n70, 147n105, 151, 188–90, 191

A Ballard of Anne Askew 190

banned books 36, 39, 47, 51, 53, 72–3, 115, 160–1

baptism 61

Barnes, Robert 17, 18, 57, 168

Basset, Anne 67

Bawmborough, Laurence 44–5

Bawmborough, Thomas 44

Baynton, Sir Edward 104

Beaufort, Lady Margaret 2

Bellanian, Nicholas 169n127

Bertano, Gurone 127

Berthelet, Thomas 97

Bible: Anne Askew 82–4, 89, 90, 105, 110–14, 117–18, 120, 168, 189; Bale writings 189; ban on 72–3; Cambridge University 19, 122; Catherine Parr 77, 97, 99, 122, 148, 150, 151, 155; Cranmer 71; Cromwell 49, 53, 72; English/Great Bible 49, 53, 54, 64, 72, 84, 99, 191;

Erasmus translation 6, 7, 36, 99, 122; European perspective 94; Gardiner on 71; Garrett 39; gospelling 53, 73; Henry VIII 56, 82; Lascelles evangelism 51; London preachers 88; Lord's Supper 62; Luther challenge 15; Ochino radical fringe 94; printing presses 35; Standish on 113, 114; Tyndale 16, 36, 41, 47, 53, 134–5; and women 84, 114, 188, 191

Bigod, Sir Francis 28–30, 39–41

Bigod, Ralph 29

Bilney, Thomas 17–18

The Bishops' Book (1537) 57

Blackstone, William 158

Blagge, Sir George 66, 126, 138, 145, 160, 164, 166, 169, 178, 179

"bluestockings" 74, 93, 186

Bocher, Joan 175

Boleyn, Anne 19, 37, 38, 40n20, 71, 77, 186

Bonner, Edmund, Bishop of London 91–2, 114, 115–20, 129, 131–3, 137, 142, 151

Book of Common Prayer 189

Book of Martyrs (Foxe) 113n70, 191

books: banned books 36, 39, 47, 51, 53, 72–3, 115, 160–1; book burnings 15, 17, 36, 132; education 6, 35–6; female authorship 93, 95, 187–8; printing press 35–6; rising circulation 107

Borough, Edward 8, 9, 10

Borough, Sir Thomas 8, 13

Bourchier, Anne 32

Bowes, Sir Martin 111n68, 112–13, 114, 170

Brandon, Catherine, Duchess of Suffolk 32, 76–7, 146, 147

Brandon, Charles, Duke of Suffolk 24, 25, 32

Bread Street Compter (prison) 114, 115

Brittayne, Christopher 84

Brooke, Elizabeth 67

Brown, Sir Humphrey 90

Bucer, Martin 106, 108

Bullinger, Henry 103, 106, 107

Burdone, Richard 176

burnings: Anne Askew 141–2, 154, 160n119, 168–71, 176–7; Barnes 18, 168; Bilney 18; Garrett and Jerome 41, 168; Henry VIII caution 79, 104, 132; Lascelles 160n119, 169–71, 176, 192; Smithfield 18, 57, 115, 168, 170, 177; Windsor Martyrs 79

Butts, Edmund 115

Butts, Sir William 66, 115

Cade, Jack 11

Caistor 23, 45, 52, 184

Caius, Thomas 100

Calvin, John 94, 95, 106

Cambridge University 5, 14, 17, 121–2, 145

canon law 15, 19, 21, 51, 82

Canterbury, Archbishop of *see* Cranmer, Thomas

Caradine, Sir Thomas 79
Cardell, Sir William 184
Cardmaker, John (aka Taylor) 88,
    128, 130
Carnbull, Henry 47
Catherine of Aragon 4, 8, 11–12,
    21, 38, 82, 101
Catherine, Queen *see* Catherine
    of Aragon; Howard, Catherine;
    Parr, Catherine
Catholicism: Act of Six Articles
    58; Anne Askew 88, 89, 90,
    92, 119; banned books 37, 99;
    Catherine Parr 97, 99, 146, 147;
    Elizabeth I reign 186; English
    Reformation 18; Erasmus 7, 99;
    Luther challenge 14, 15; Mary
    Tudor reign 176; mass 61, 62,
    89, 108–10, 117–18, 127, 138,
    175, 176; Ochino radical fringe
    94; religious conflict 41, 49, 57,
    78, 88, 127
Cecil, William 187
Cervington [?] 40, 41
Chantries Act 121, 145
Chapel Royal 78, 79
Chapuys, Eustace 67, 73, 125
Charles II, King 1
Charles V, Emperor 13, 36, 81,
    92, 127
Cheke, John 146
Christianity 16, 57, 82, 94, 100,
    107, 112
Christina of Denmark 77
Church of England 19, 21–3, 55,
    118, 176
Clarke, James 44–5

Clement VII, Pope 21
Clinton, Anne 185–6
Clinton, Edward Fiennes, Earl of
    Lincoln 32, 185
Colchester burnings 132
Colet, John 35
Colonna, Vittoria, Marchioness of
    Pescara 95
Commentaries on the Laws of England
    (Blackstone) 158
communion 89, 115, 127, 176
Compter (prison) 114, 115
confession 111–12, 114, 119–20
confirmation 16
conversion narratives 42, 187
Cooke, Anthony 146
Council of Trent 99
"Cousin Britain" 115
Coverdale, Miles 17, 184
Cranmer, Thomas, Archbishop
    of Canterbury: attacks on 145,
    155, 163; becomes Archbishop
    19; Cambridge University 17;
    Canterbury heresy hunt 79–81;
    and Catherine Howard 65; and
    Catherine Parr 95, 100, 146;
    Cromwell's fall 58; and Edward
    Askew 19; English prayer book
    100; and Germain Gardiner
    80–1, 95; Great Bible 64, 71,
    72; influence of 180; Joan
    Bocher trial 175; Lincolnshire
    Rebellion 48; Lutheranism 60;
    mass doctrine 89, 108, 138,
    175–6; Ochino invitation 95;
    and radicals 61; and Stephen
    Gardiner 78, 80, 163

Crome, Dr Edward 59–60, 88,
    104–5, 128–30, 131, 137,
    139–40
Cromwell, Thomas: Act of
    Supremacy 20; and Anne of
    Cleves 55, 57, 60; Bale writings
    188–9; and Bigod 29, 40; death
    of 52, 57, 124, 144; evangelical
    reform 21–2, 23, 29; fall of 57–
    9, 64, 78, 80, 81, 145, 155, 157,
    163, 168; Great Bible 53, 54, 72,
    99; "great ruffling" 31; industry
    of 54; influence of 180; and
    Lascelles 51; and Latimer 30–1;
    Lincolnshire Rebellion 24, 48;
    promoter of reformists 66;
    religious policy 47; and Richard
    Rich 126; rise to power 19, 20;
    Rotherham heretics 49; and
    Sir William Askew 44, 46, 52;
    Southwell promotion 136
Culpepper, Thomas 65

Dalyson, Lady Elizabeth 184
Dalyson, William 46
d'Annebaut, Admiral Claude 127
Darcy, Lord 26
Dare, Christopher 111–12
Day, George, Bishop of
    Chichester 97
Denny, Sir Anthony 66, 115, 177
Denny, Lady 156, 157
Dentière, Marie 188
Dereham, Francis 63–4
de Selve, Ambassador 177–8
Dighton, Robert 46
Dissolution 32

divorce 65, 82–3, 91
Don river 47
Drapper, Mr 48
Dudley, John, Viscount Lisle 66,
    77, 87, 124, 125, 138, 139, 157,
    177, 178
Dudley, Lady 146
"Duke of Exeter's daughter" (the
    rack) 158–9, 164, 165, 168
Dymock, Sir Thomas 44

education 4–7, 16, 29, 35–6, 93
Edward the Confessor 178
Edward IV, King 2, 3
Edward, Prince (later King
    Edward VI) 74, 101, 122–3,
    128, 162, 176, 180, 183
Eland, Sir Edward 51
Elizabeth, Princess (later Queen
    Elizabeth I) 76n41, 95, 101–2,
    122, 147, 182–3, 184, 186
English Bible 49, 53, 54, 64, 72,
    84, 99, 191
English church 19, 21–3, 55, 118,
    176
English Prayer Book 100, 108
English Reformation see
    Reformation
Equicola, Mario 5
Erasmus, Desiderius: Cambridge
    University 14, 17, 122; Catherine
    Parr 99, 122; education of
    women 5–6; *Novum Instrumentum*
    6–7; *Paraphrases* 17, 36, 99–100,
    122; as reformer 35–6
Esther, Queen 76
eucharist 89, 107, 109, 111, 167

executions 30, 49, 57–8, 168 *see also* burnings

faith 15, 50, 148–50, 151
Farrago omnium fere rerum theologicarum (Lambert) 36, 37
female authorship 93, 95, 187–8
Ferdinand II of Aragon 92
Field of the Cloth of Gold 13
The First Examination of Anne Askew, lately martyred in Smithfield 190
Fisher, Bishop John 97
Fitzwilliam, Lady 156
Fleet prison 79
food supplies 87
Foxe, John: *Acts and Monuments of the Christian Religion* 111n68, 144n103, 168, 169n127, 170, 190; on Anne Askew 110n68, 113n70, 119–20, 155, 159, 168, 169n127, 170, 190–1; *Book of Martyrs* 113n70, 191; on Catherine Parr 144, 154, 160; on Henry VIII 80; and John Bale 190; on Norwich arrests 141
France 81, 85–7, 92, 103, 124, 125, 127
Francis I, King of France 93, 125
The Freedom of the Christian Man (Luther) 15
free will 122, 191
Furnival's Inn 51

Gardiner, Germain 80, 81, 95
Gardiner, Stephen, Bishop of Winchester: Act of Six Articles 58, 78; and Anne Askew 137, 138, 142, 154, 191; Bale writings 191; and Catherine Howard 57; and Catherine Parr 144, 145–6, 154, 155, 162–3; and Cranmer 78, 80, 163; Dudley allegedly slaps 178; faction fighting 124–8; on Great Bible 72; Henry VIII marriage to Catherine Parr 78; Henry VIII's caution 162–3, 179; and Jane Wriothesley 95; Lady Suffolk's dog 77, 146; on Lascelles 130–1; religious conflict 88; Rich and Wriothesley 126, 135, 142, 154, 163; on war and economy 86; Windsor Martyrs 79
Garrett, Thomas 39, 41, 168
Gentlemen Pensioners 3
Gerrard, Thomas 57
Goldsmith, Francis 75–6
Gonzaga, Giulia 94
Gospel 76, 137
gospelling 53, 73
Great Bible 49, 53, 54, 64, 72, 84, 99, 191
"great ruffling" 28, 31, 32, 43
Green, Maud *see* Parr, Maud
Green, Sir Thomas 3
Grey, Lady Jane 183
Grove, John 176
Guildhall 91, 120, 141

Hadlam, John 140, 169
Hall, Edward 85, 115
Hall, Mary (née Lascelles) 50, 52, 63, 65–6

Hampton Court 13, 73, 78, 102
Hansard, Elizabeth *see* Askew,
  Elizabeth (née Hansard)
Hansard family 13–14
Hanschey, Robert (alias Smith)
  45, 46
Hanseatic League 47
Harmon, Edmund 79
Hastings, Sir Thomas 184
Haynes, Simon 79
Heath, Nicholas 129
Hemsley, John 169
Heneage, Sir John 46
Henry VI, King 11
Henry VII, King 2–3, 11
Henry VIII, King: and Anne
  Askew 155–6, 159–60, 190;
  Anne Boleyn marriage 19,
  40n20, 71, 77, 186; Anne of
  Cleves marriage 54–5, 57;
  banned books 99, 100; Bertano
  reforms 127; and Bigod 40;
  book burnings 132; burnings
  appeals 177; Catherine Howard
  marriage 57, 63–6, 77; Catherine
  of Aragon marriage 4, 18, 21;
  Catherine Parr investigation
  144–5, 151, 154–5, 159–60,
  161–3; Catherine Parr marriage
  67–8, 73–8, 92–3, 95, 99–101,
  123, 151; Catherine Parr
  writings 97, 99; Chantries Act
  121; and Cranmer 19, 80–1;
  and Cromwell's fall 57–9; death
  of 100, 128, 179, 181, 190;
  divorce 82; early days of reign
  3–4; and Edward Seymour

178; Erasmus *Paraphrases* 99;
  failing health 71, 128; Field
  of the Cloth of Gold 13;
  and Gardiner 155, 179; Great
  Bible 53, 56, 72, 191; heresy
  persecutions 62, 108; influence
  and impact 71; *The King's Book*
  72, 119; and Lascelles 63–5,
  137; Lincolnshire Rebellion
  24–5; Luther's theology 36;
  mass doctrine 108, 127; Neville
  service 10; Pilgrimage of Grace
  26–7; political conflict 66–7,
  123–5, 177–8; reform and revolt
  26–7, 29–32; Reformation
  origins 16, 18, 34, 37, 40, 180,
  191; religious discord 55–9, 103;
  sweating sickness 7; war with
  France 12–13, 81, 92–3, 103,
  121; and William Askew 12–13;
  Windsor Martyrs 79
Herbert, Anne (née Parr) 4, 7, 32,
  55, 73, 76, 88, 154
Herbert, William 32, 55, 66, 75
Hercy, Elizabeth 50
Hercy, Humphrey 50
Hercy, Sir John 51
heresy: Act of Six Articles 57,
  58, 176; Anne Askew 89–92,
  105, 141, 154, 155, 165–71,
  176; banned books 15, 39, 132;
  Bocher trial 175; Bonner 132;
  Catherine Parr 145, 150, 155;
  Council records 140; Cranmer
  19, 78–9, 175; Crome 104–5,
  130; evangelical heresy 17;
  faction fighting 126–7, 131–2;

Gardiner 162; Great Bible
72; Henry VIII view 55, 57,
132, 145, 155, 162; Huick 130;
Lascelles 51, 89–90, 130–1,
166; Latimer 130; Lollardy 62;
Luther challenge 15, 36; mass
doctrine 89, 108; Richard Rich
126, 136; Rotherham heretics
47–8; Sir William Askew's view
45; sociological composition
16–17; Windsor Martyrs 78–9
Hertford, Earl of *see* Seymour,
Edward
Hertford, Lady 76, 77, 88, 95, 156,
157
Heywood, John 37
Hilles, Richard 59
A Historie [.] (Sir Edward
Ayscough) 133, 134
Hoby, Sir Philip 79
Holbein, Hans 55
Holborn law schools 48
Holden, Thomas 48
holy communion 89, 115, 127, 176
Holy Spirit 94, 110, 112
Hooper, John 103–4
Howard, Agnes, Dowager
Duchess of Norfolk 52, 63
Howard, Catherine 32, 52, 57,
63–7, 77, 155
Howard, Thomas, Duke of
Norfolk: Act of Six Articles 58;
Anne Askew execution 169; and
Anne Boleyn 20; and Catherine
Howard 57, 65; condemned to
death 179; Council records 141;
and Crome 139; English Bible

64; faction fighting 124, 126;
reform and revolt 26, 27, 30,
31; and Richard Rich 135; and
Seymour family 126, 178
Huick, Dr Robert 128, 129, 130,
131, 135
Hull 28, 30, 31, 47
humanism 4, 5, 14, 16, 57

Imitation of Christ (Thomas à
Kempis) 101
Index of Banned Books 99, 115
infant baptism 61
inflation 85
Ingram, William 47
Inquisition 95, 158
The Instruction of a Christian Woman
(Vives) 7
Ipswich college 29
Italy 94–5

Jane Seymour, Queen *see* Seymour,
Jane
Jansz, Anna 106
Jerome, William 40, 41, 42, 57, 168
Julich, Duke of Cleves 55
justification by faith 42, 60

The King's Book (*The Necessary
Doctrine and Erudition for Any
Christian Man*) 72, 119
Kirby, John 132
Knyvett, Sir Anthony 158, 159,
160
Kyme, Anne *see* Askew, Anne
Kyme, Thomas 43–4, 53, 63, 83,
133, 135, 136

Lambert, François 36, 37

The Lamentation of a Sinner (Catherine Parr) 41, 42, 146–51, 154, 187

Lancaster, House of 1, 11

Lascelles, George 50

Lascelles, John: and Anne Askew 84, 88–90, 109, 160n119, 163, 166, 169–71, 176; arrest and imprisonment 130–1, 135, 137–8, 145, 163–4, 166; and Catherine Howard 63, 64–5; and Crome 128, 129, 131; and Cromwell 51; death of 160n119, 169–71, 176, 192; mass doctrine 109; upbringing 50

Lascelles, Mary (sister of John) 50, 52, 63, 65–6

Lascelles, Mary (descendant of John) 192

Lateran Council 99

The Later Examination 190

Latimer, Baron (John Neville) 10, 26–32, 39, 67, 73, 74

Latimer, Lady Catherine *see* Parr, Catherine

Latimer, Hugh 17–18, 48, 59, 88, 107, 108, 130, 135

Latimer, Margaret 29

Lee, Archbishop Edward 26

Lefèvre d'Étaples, Jacques 94

Lenton Priory 50

libertarianism 16

Lincoln 83, 84, 118

Lincoln Castle 45

Lincolnshire 8–9, 13, 43, 47, 186

Lincolnshire Rebellion 23–5, 48, 53

Lisle, Lady 76, 77, 88, 95

Lisle, Lord *see* Dudley, John

A Litel Treatise ageynst the mutterynge of some papists in corners (Swinnerton) 37

literacy 35

literature 132

"Little Germany" (White Horse Inn, Cambridge) 17

Lollardy 47, 62, 114, 168

London 65, 84–8

London, Bishop of *see* Bonner, Edmund; Tunstall, Cuthbert

London, Dr John 78–9, 81

Lord's Supper 61, 62, 107, 108, 141, 163, 165

Loud, Archdeacon 113n70

Louthe, John 169

Lucas, Mr, of Colchester 140–1

Lukine, Thomas 90–1, 92

Luther, Martin: *The Address to the Christian Nobility of the German Nation* 15; *The Babylonian Captivity of the Church* 15; book burnings 17; Catherine Parr's writings 42, 148; challenge to Catholicism 14, 15, 36; and Erasmus 122; *The Freedom of the Christian Man* 15; Margaret of Navarre 94; mass doctrine 61, 107, 139; "95 Theses" 14, 42; Ochino 94; *On Good Works* 15; Reformation origins 8, 17

Lutheranism 39, 60, 106–7

Magna Carta 158

Manipulus Curatorum (the "Curate's

Manual") 35
Manox, Henry 63
Marbeck, John 79
Margaret of Anjou 11
Margaret of Navarre 93–4, 102,
    147
Marillac, Charles de 58–9
Markham of Cottam, Sir John 48,
    49–50
Marot, Clément 94
martyrdom 17, 105–6, 165
Mary of Guise 128
Mary, Princess (later Queen Mary
    I, Mary Tudor): becomes queen
    176; and Catherine Parr 38,
    73, 100, 101, 183; education 7;
    Erasmus *Paraphrases* translation
    100; and Prince Edward 123;
    reign as queen 76, 100, 115,
    132, 136, 176, 190; and Thomas
    Seymour 182
mass 61, 62, 89, 108–10, 117–18,
    127, 138, 175, 176
May, William 129
memorialism 110
*The Merry Play between the Pardoner
    and the Friar* (Heywood) 37
Mirror of the Sinful Soul (*Miroir de
    L'âme Pécheresse*) (Margaret of
    Navarre) 94, 102, 147
monasteries 22, 23, 29, 32, 47, 85
monasticism 15, 16, 23, 26, 39, 49
More, Margaret 5
More, Thomas 2, 5, 21, 36–7, 42,
    47, 126, 144
Morice, Ralph 135–6
Morice, William 135, 136, 140

Musgrave, Sir William 30–1
mysticism 94

Naples 94
*The Necessary Doctrine and Erudition
    for Any Christian Man* (*The King's
    Book*) 72, 119
Neville, Anthony 51
Neville, John, Baron Latimer 10,
    26–8, 30–2, 39, 67, 73, 74
Neville, Margaret 10
Newark 186
Newgate Prison 136, 140, 142,
    163–4, 168
New Learning 18, 29, 38, 40, 51,
    64, 115
New Testament: Bible on women
    188; Erasmus translation 6, 17,
    36, 99; Rotherham heretics 47,
    48; Tyndale version 16, 36, 41,
    47, 53, 134–5; Windsor Martyrs
    79
New World 47
"95 Theses" (Luther) 14, 42
Norfolk, Duchess of (Agnes
    Howard) 52, 63
Norfolk, Duke of *see* Howard,
    Thomas
Norwich 18, 141
Nottinghamshire 13, 47, 186
Novum Instrumentum (Erasmus) 6–7
Nun Cotham Priory 14
Nuthall 12, 14, 19

Ochino, Bernadino 94–5
On Divine and Human Justice
    (Zwingli) 16

On Good Works (Luther) 15
On True and False Religion (Zwingli) 16
ordination 16
Our Lady of Walsingham shrine 4
Oxford 2, 29, 39

Paget, William 86, 87, 138–9
pamphlets 36, 39, 107
papacy: Bertano meeting 127; Bigod 29–30; Cranmer as Archbishop 19; English Reformation 191; Henry VIII 18, 19, 20, 29–30, 39, 71, 127, 191; Luther challenge 8, 14, 15; monasteries 23, 29
papalism 49, 56, 60, 97, 110
Parable of the Wicked Mammon (Tyndale) 37
Paraphrases (Erasmus) 17, 36, 99–100, 122
Parr, Anne (sister of Catherine) *see* Herbert, Anne
Parr, Catherine: and Anne Askew 85, 88–9, 151; appearance 74; birth of 4; on Cambridge University 121–2; conversion 34–5; correspondence 67–8, 74; death of 183–4; education 4, 35, 38, 41, 93; English Reformation 186–7; Erasmus translation 99–100; faith and beliefs 39, 93, 97, 122; family life 101–2, 122–3, 183; in historical perspective 180, 181, 186–7, 192; investigation of 58, 144–51, 154–5, 159–63;

and Jane Wriothesley 95–6; *The Lamentation of a Sinner* 41, 42, 146–51, 154, 187; Lutheranism 42; marriage to Edward Borough 8–10; marriage to Henry VIII 67–8, 73–8, 92–3, 181, 186, 187; marriage to John Neville (Baron Latimer) 10, 27–33, 39, 67, 73, 74; marriage to Thomas Seymour 181–3, 187; New Learning 38, 41; "Prayer for the King" 97; *Prayers or Meditations* 101, 102, 187; and Prince Edward 122–3; *Psalms or Prayers taken out of Holy scripture* 97–9; Queen Esther comparison 75–6; religious influences 41–3, 60, 94–5; at Stowe Manor 55; upbringing 1, 7–9; writings 41–2, 74, 93, 97–102, 138, 146–51, 154, 180–1, 187–8
Parr, Elizabeth (mother of Thomas Parr) 2
Parr, Maud (née Green) (mother of Catherine) 3–4, 7–8, 9, 38
Parr, Sir Thomas (father of Catherine) 2–4, 7, 8
Parr, William, Baron of Kendal (father of Thomas Parr) 2
Parr, Sir William (uncle of Catherine) 8, 31
Parr, William, Baron of Kendal (brother of Catherine): and Anne Askew 138; and Anne Bourchier 32; and Catherine Parr correspondence 67–8, 147; and Duke of Norfolk

31; and Elizabeth Brooke 67; Lord Warden appointment 75; peerage 32; in royal entourage 55, 66, 73; upbringing 4, 8

Parsons, Robert 175n131

Paul, St 42, 77, 82, 114, 117, 134, 152

Peasants' War 61

penance 14, 16

pilgrimage 22

Pilgrimage of Grace 25–7, 29, 32

Pilgrim Fathers 186

plague 84

Pole, John de la 11

popes *see* papacy

prayer books 100, 108, 176, 189

"Prayer for the King" (Catherine Parr) 97

Prayers or Meditations (Catherine Parr) 101, 102, 187

preaching 18, 29, 40, 87–8, 114

priesthood 29, 40, 111–12

printing presses 15, 17, 35

Protestantism 34, 37, 41, 60, 90, 176, 180, 186

Psalms or Prayers taken out of Holy scripture (Catherine Parr) 97–9

Puritanism 47, 186

Pylley, Thomas 47

quests (inquests) 91, 110–11

Rabelais, François 94

racking 158–9, 164, 165, 168

Radcliffe, Anne, Countess of Sussex 76, 77, 156

radicalism: Anne Askew 88, 106,

110; Cambridge University 14, 17; Catherine Parr writings 150–1; Luther 36; Nottinghamshire 47; religious discord 60, 62

reason 122

Rede Me and Be Notte Wrothe 37

Redman, John 129

Reformation: Act of Six Articles 58; Anne Askew 34, 106, 176; Bigod 40; Bowes 180; Cambridge University 17, 18; Catherine Parr 34, 176, 186; Cromwell 49; Elizabeth I reign 186; English Bible 191; Erasmus 99; Henry VIII 18, 21, 37, 74, 82, 180, 191; Luther 8, 14; Ochino radical fringe 94; origins of 8, 14, 37; Reformation Parliament 20; spread of 14, 18, 19

relics 49

religion: Act for the Advancement of True Religion 57, 72, 84, 99; Act of Six Articles 57; banned books 72, 132; change and conflict 16, 19, 60, 93, 103–4; conversion 34; Cromwell 21–2; faction fighting 124–8; Henry VIII 21, 163; Luther challenge 15–16, 122; mass doctrine 108–10; Protestantism 186; radicalism 14, 47, 88, 110, 128, 150–1; religious truth 39; royal Council 124

Renaissance 2, 5, 14, 16, 35

Revel, Tristram 37

Rich, Sir Richard 113n70, 126,

135–6, 142–3, 154–5, 159–60, 163, 165, 189–90
Richard III, King 2, 8
Richmond, Duchess of 126
Richmond, Duke of 8
Ridley, Nicholas 129, 175
Rotherham 47–8
"ruffling" 28, 31, 32, 43
Russell, Lord John 160, 169, 170
Rye House 1, 4
Ryrie, Alec 157

sacrament 61, 108, 111, 115, 118–19, 137–8, 140, 141, 167
sacramentarianism 61, 128, 137, 138
Saddlers' Hall 110
salvation 15, 94–5, 100, 146, 153, 167, 188
Sawtry, Joan 90–1, 92
Scarborough 30, 31
Schmalkalde League 49
Scotland 81, 86, 87, 92–3
Scripture *see* Bible
Selby Abbey 14
Senes, William 47, 48–9
Seymour, Anne, Duchess of Somerset 182–3
Seymour, Edward, Earl of Hertford (Duke of Somerset, Lord Protector) 66, 77, 81, 124–7, 139, 157, 160n119, 177–9, 181–3, 187
Seymour, Jane 32, 54
Seymour, Thomas 74, 77, 126, 146, 181–3, 184, 187
Shaxton, Nicholas 88, 105, 132,

135, 137, 141, 142, 170
Sheffield Castle 48
Shrewsbury, Earl of 26, 30, 48
shrines 22, 49
Six Articles Act *see* Act of Six Articles
Smithfield burnings 18, 57, 115, 168, 170, 177
Snape Castle 10, 11, 27, 28
Soke of Caistor 184
Somerset, Duchess of (Anne Seymour) 182–3
Somerset, Duke of *see* Seymour, Edward
South Kelsey Hall 9, 13, 14, 17, 18, 20, 23–4, 134
Southwell, Sir Richard 113n70, 126, 136, 179
Spirituali 94
Standish, Dr John 113, 114, 115, 116, 118
Steelyard raid 47
Stowe Manor 32, 55
Strasbourg 61, 106
Strype, John 91
Sudeley Castle 183
Suffolk, Duchess of (Catherine Brandon) 32, 76–7, 146, 147
Suffolk, Duke of (Charles Brandon) 24, 25, 32
Surrey, Earl of 126, 136, 178–9
sweating sickness 7, 13
Swenson, Ralph 50
Swinnerton, Thomas 39

taxation 85
Taylor, John (satirist) 191

Taylor, John (vicar) 88, 128, 130
Testwood, Robert 79
Thomas à Kempis 101
Thornton Abbey 14
Throckmorton, Nicholas 166, 169
torture 158–9, 164–6, 168 Tower
    of London: Anne Askew
    113n70, 143, 154–60, 164;
    Blagge 138, 145; Catherine
    Howard 66; Henry VIII 145;
    Huick 131; Lascelles 131;
    Latimer 31, 130; Norfolk and
    Surrey 179; racking 158, 164;
    Thomas Green 3
Traheron, Bartholomew 107–8
transubstantiation 15, 58, 108,
    114, 137
treason 58, 65, 81, 97, 155, 178,
    184
*A Treatise concerning Impropriations
    of Benefices* (Francis Bigod) 40
Trent river 47
Tunstall, Cuthbert, Bishop of
    London 2, 5, 7, 18, 36, 51
Tyndale, William: Anne Askew
    134–5; *Answer to More* 42;
    Catherine Parr writings 97;
    New Testament 16, 36, 41, 47,
    53, 134–5; *Parable of the Wicked
    Mammon* 37; radicalism 62
Tyrrwhit, Sir Robert 45, 46, 52

Udall, Nicholas 99–100

Valdes, Juan 94
Valor Ecclesiasticus 22
Vaux, Sir Nicholas 2

Vives, Juan Luis 7
Vulgate of St Jerome 7, 36

Wadloe, Master 91
Warne, John 177
wars 12–13, 81, 85–7, 92–3, 121,
    124–5
"Wars of the Roses" 1
Waterloo, Battle of 71
Weldon, Sir Thomas 79
Wellington, Duke of 71
Wendy, Dr 161
White, Christopher 141, 142
Whitehead, William 88
White Horse Inn, Cambridge 17
Williams, John 9n3
Willoughby, Catherine *see*
    Brandon, Catherine
wills 50
Wilton House 75
Winchester, Bishop of *see*
    Gardiner, Stephen
Windsor 13, 26, 78–9
Windsor Castle 26
Windsor Martyrs 79
Wisdom, Robert 132–3
witches 158
Wittenberg 8, 14, 42, 61, 107
Wolsey, Thomas, Cardinal 13, 15,
    19, 29, 36, 37, 124, 144
women: and Bible 84, 114, 188,
    191; education of 5–6, 7, 16, 35,
    93; female authorship 93, 95,
    187–8; racking 158
Woodville family 3
Worley (court page) 128, 131
Wright, Christopher 140

Wriothesley, Jane 95–6
Wriothesley, Thomas: and Anne
  Askew 91, 154, 156–60, 165,
  169, 170, 189–90; Bale writings
  189–90; and Catherine Parr 146,
  162, 163; on economy 85–6;
  and Henry VIII 163; heresy
  persecutions 126, 135; racking
  158–9, 165; religious conflict 87
Wrottesley, William 12

Wyatt, Sir Thomas 66, 71, 104
Wycklyffes Wycket 62
Wycliffe, John 62

York, House of 1, 2, 3, 11

Zurich 61, 106, 108
Zwingli, Huldrych 16, 61, 110
Zwinglianism 108, 138, 168, 175

Lightning Source UK Ltd.
Milton Keynes UK
UKHW02n1525190818
327414UK00003BA/227/P